RAISING AN EXPLOSIVE CHILD LIKE A PRO

Parenting OCD, ADHD, and ODD Children With Empathy. A Proven Path to Combating Overwhelm, Avoiding Angry Outbursts, and Raising a Happy Child.

G.G. GRAYHAVEN

Prodigal Recordings LLC

DISCLAIMER

This book is intended to provide tools and exercises designed to assist in improving communication and relationships within families. It is important for readers to understand that this book does not offer a quick fix for families experiencing explosive behaviors or deep-seated relational issues. The strategies and insights presented herein are meant to serve as guidance and support for those seeking to enhance their familial connections and communication skills.

The content of this book is based on the author's professional experience, research, and insights into family dynamics. While these tools and exercises have been beneficial for many, they do not guarantee resolution of all family conflicts or behavioral challenges. The effectiveness of the strategies outlined in this book depends on the commitment, effort, and context of each individual family's situation.

Readers are encouraged to approach this book with an open mind and a willingness to engage in the process of learning and applying these tools. It may also be beneficial to seek professional assistance for specific issues that are beyond the scope of this book. The author and publisher make no claims to the efficacy of this book in treating severe psychological disorders or replacing professional therapeutic interventions.

By reading this book, you acknowledge and agree that the author and publisher are not responsible for the outcomes of applying the strategies contained within. This book is not a substitute for professional advice or treatment. Any reliance you place on the information in this book is strictly at your own risk.

NAVIGATE YOUR JOURNEY

Welcome to a book designed with flexibility in mind, recognizing that every reader's journey and needs are unique. This is not a book that demands to be read from cover to cover in a linear fashion. Instead, we invite you to jump in at any chapter that speaks to you, at any moment that feels right.

Whether you're seeking immediate guidance on a particular challenge or looking for insights into a specific aspect of family communication, this book is structured to accommodate your needs. Feel free to explore the chapters in any order that resonates with you. Each section stands on its own, offering valuable tools and exercises that are effective independently of the rest.

Dive into what interests you the most, revisit sections as needed, and use this book as a resource to refer to time and time again. Your path through these pages is yours to choose, making your reading experience as personalized and impactful as possible.

CONTENTS

INTRODUCTION

A shout rings out above the rumble of general party chatter. Marcy looks up from the kitchen sink. Through the window, she can see her daughter, Lillah, and her cousins by the pool. Lillah is stiff, her body tight with characteristic rage. One of the boys is refusing to play the game that Lillah wants. He isn't being rude, simply saying "No."

Marcy feels herself shrink from the inside out. She recognizes Lillah's body language as intimately as she recognizes her own reflection. A storm is coming. Marcy is too far away to intervene and redirect her daughter. In her mind's eye, she can already see the poor boy being pushed into the pool; she can hear the shouts of rage and see the stomping of Lillah's little feet.

As she starts to move to the open kitchen door, filled with desperation and a shame she could never put words to, she suddenly stops.

Lillah has turned away from the boy—even in her rage. Her eyes are squeezed shut, and her lips are pursed as she takes each breath nice and slow.

Marcy watches, transfixed, as her explosive daughter takes the steps to calm herself down.

Most of the tension leaves those tiny shoulders, and the fists at her sides relax. Lillah looks up and meets the gaze of her loving mother across the garden and smiles questioningly.

That feeling of desperation softens into one of pride. Marcy beams at her daughter and gives her the thumbs up, which Lillah returns. With the support of her mother, Lillah takes one more breath and turns back to her cousins to rejoin the game, calmer and not explosive.

Marcy and Lillah have been on a long journey of learning about explosive behavior. Together, they had some really dark moments, but together, they navigated the chaos and discovered strategies to help them find harmony instead.

Perhaps you have felt like Marcy did just now, desperate and ashamed of your child's behavior. But you have picked up this book, *Raising an Explosive Child Like a Pro*, which means you know that there is another way.

THE JOURNEY AHEAD

This book is designed for parents, grandparents, and caregivers of children with OCD, ADHD, and ODD. It will also be useful for other family members of the kiddo who are having explosive behavior. It is here to help you navigate the complexities of parenting a child with one or more of these conditions with empathy, effective discipline, and balanced family dynamics.

Throughout this book, you are going to realize the importance of your own behavior while nurturing your child's behavior. After all, parents truly are the key role models in their children's lives. We set the standard for how they behave. It is up to us to praise them when they deserve it and guide them when they are struggling.

Often, parents of explosive children feel isolated; they feel as though they may be responsible for their child's behavior because they have been too "soft" or too passive, or even that there is something "wrong" with their child.

Having worked in the mental health field with at-risk kids and teens for over 15 years, I have a wealth of experience and understanding in managing and nurturing explosive children. I have hands-on experience, have studied applied behavior analysis, and worked toward my board certified behavioral analysis certificate.

If you are coming to this book feeling hopeless and alone, please know that it will not always be this way. There is nothing wrong with you or your child, and together, you can transform your relationship and your child's explosive behavior. This is not a space of judgment; here, you will find understanding, kinship, and support.

You are encouraged to engage with all the exercises, case studies, and reflections that you find throughout this book; they are there to help you understand your child and to learn practical skills to help you manage stressful situations as they arise and even to prevent them from occurring in the first place.

The key themes and topics covered in the book include:

- Understanding explosive behavior in children and its impacts.
- Identifying underlying causes like emotional dysregulation, communication barriers, and neurodevelopmental factors.
- Effective parenting strategies like positive reinforcement, teaching emotional intelligence, and tailored behavioral therapies.

- Building emotional resilience and coping skills in both parents and children.
- Managing the educational and social challenges these children face.
- Creating a supportive home environment conducive to positive behavior.
- Maintaining family relationships and dynamics.
- Looking toward the future with a hopeful outlook based on real-life success stories.

UNDERSTANDING EXPLOSIVE CHILDREN

According to Dr. Ross Greene (2021), "'explosive' is just a descriptive term for kids who become frustrated far more easily and more often and communicate their frustration in ways that are far more extreme (screaming, swearing, spitting, hitting, kicking, biting, cutting, destroying property) than 'ordinary' kids."

Defining the "Explosive Child"

Managing explosive behaviors in children can often leave parents feeling burned out, drained, and desperate. Meltdowns in children with OCD, ADHD, and ODD are not the same as the kind of tantrums experienced by other children. Explosive behavior is often triggered by sensory overload and overwhelm rather than by the typical frustrations a young child experiences, such as not getting what they want (Bennie, 2016). Because explosive behavior is different, it requires a whole different skill set, which can be absolutely exhausting for a parent as well as the child experiencing it.

In order to effectively deal with this kind of behavior, it is imperative to understand the underlying causes. There are often complex psychological, neurological, and environmental factors driving these outbursts. These children are not just having a "temper tantrum," so the techniques one might use to deal with that do not apply here. It is also important to recognize that explosive behavior is not "just a phase," and we should never assume a child can control it. We have to expand the tools in our parenting toolbox and learn to respond in a way that helps to redirect or minimize the situation, and at the same time, we need to help the child learn healthy emotional regulation.

The Role of Diagnosis

Three diagnoses commonly associated with explosive behavior in children are obsessive-compulsive disorder (OCD), attention-deficit/hyperactivity disorder (ADHD), and oppositional defiant disorder (ODD).

- **OCD:** Involves unwanted and intrusive thoughts that make up the "obsessive" part of this condition, which trigger repetitive behaviors and are also known as "compulsions." OCD can result in intensely distressing feelings if these rituals or routines are not performed (Mayo Clinic Staff, 2023).
- **ADHD/ADD:** ADHD is a neurodevelopmental disorder characterized by inattentiveness, impulsivity, and hyperactivity. It was formerly known as attention-deficit disorder (ADD) but expanded to reflect the importance of the hyperactivity component (Cleveland Clinic, 2017).
- **ODD:** ODD is defined by an ongoing pattern of hostile and defiant behavior toward peers, parents, teachers, and other authority figures (Johns Hopkins Medicine, n.d.).

All three conditions are known to influence children's ability to regulate emotions, control impulses, and modulate behavior. This often translates into extreme emotional reactivity and explosive reactions to what may appear as minor triggers to a casual observer.

Without understanding the driving diagnoses, parents may resort to anger or punishment, which only exacerbates negative behaviors.

While tempting, self-diagnosing a child can also contribute to parental anxiety as well as strain the parent-child relationship. A professional clinical evaluation is extremely important to accurately identify any diagnoses contributing to the "explosive" episodes that your child is experiencing.

Having a formal diagnosis will help you to get the help that your child needs at home, at school, and in the wider community. Only an experienced diagnostician can tell you whether OCD, ADHD, ODD, or other conditions may be at play, allowing parents to better understand and assist their struggling child.

The Impact on Family Life

The frequent emotional outbursts and explosive behavior of a child with one of these conditions can have an immense impact on families. Parents often feel overwhelmed, confused, and frustrated while constantly feeling as though they have to "walk on eggshells" to avoid triggering another episode. This can also disrupt the family routines, having an impact on planned activities and even your job.

Coping with these diagnoses can really strain relationships within the family. The relationship between the parents can be strained and full of resentment and blame; there might be arguments about differing ideas on discipline and coping with the behavior. It can also be detrimental to sibling relationships, causing resentment there as the explosive child absorbs all the time and attention—even if that attention is negative.

All the while, parents will slowly begin to neglect themselves amidst the stress of managing meltdowns. Burnout and emotional exhaustion are common in parents of children with these diagnoses. This is such an integral topic that we will explore during the course of this book. In order to be the best version of themselves, remain patient and calm, and offer the support that their child needs, parents have to learn how to prioritize self-care.

SETTING REALISTIC EXPECTATIONS

If you came to this book looking for a quick fix for your child's behavior, you are going to be sadly disappointed. These conditions and this behavior require long-term management. The skills you are going to learn are almost like lifestyle changes; you may have to completely rewrite your discipline structure and everything you think you know about parenting.

Remember, your child is not a problem to be "fixed." Instead, view it as their behavior that needs to be managed. There are two tools that are going to be so important for you along the way, and they are patience and resilience. It's important to ditch any blame or shame you might be carrying for yourself, your partner, or your kid(s)—those feelings aren't going to get you anywhere!

Your expectations may very well be holding you back; every child develops differently, and it's our responsibility to meet our children where they are instead of expecting them to align with whatever social, emotional, and neurological goals you have in mind for them. And it's not only your expectations that need to be managed— school and community expectations also need to be explored.

The Power of Small Wins

As mentioned, this is not going to be an overnight success. Think back to Marcy and Lillah; it took them years to get to a point where Lillah could self-regulate on her own. Their success was quite simply down to the culmination of all the small wins they had along the way. Small wins truly are the building blocks to success in resolving explosive behaviors.

The key is to set and reinforce small, realistic, and achievable goals. For example, let's say your child is prone to interrupting. You teach them to place their hand on your arm when they need to speak and to wait patiently. At first, they may touch your arm but continue to interrupt. Instead of expecting them to get it right the first time, you instead praise them for putting their hand on your arm. The next time they want to interrupt, they may place their hand on your arm and be able to remain quiet for ten seconds. When they interrupt this time, you praise them for touching your arm and for staying quiet for ten seconds. Over time, they manage to touch your arm and wait for one whole minute. This cycle continues, and you praise every small milestone until, eventually, they are able to let you finish your conversation without interrupting. It is in this way that small wins contribute to larger progress and less stress for both you and your child.

Avoiding Common Pitfalls

The journey to overcoming explosive behavior is not always going to be a smooth one. Pitfalls and mistakes are going to look slightly different for each family and each situation, but there are some common mistakes to be aware of, which should help you to avoid them: inconsistency and unrealistic expectations.

Deciding to set rules and standards means following through on them, which is especially important for children with these diagnoses. Inconsistent rewards and punishments can lead to confusion and anxiety and can actually fuel the unwanted behavior.

As mentioned, it is so important to meet your child where they are so that you don't set them up for failure on this journey. Make sure that any expectations you set for things like homework are age- and developmentally-appropriate. In the same way that a baby cannot walk until they are developmentally ready, your explosive child cannot simply overcome obstacles until they are ready.

Your support network is going to be integral in helping you to avoid these pitfalls. The other parent, friends, and family can help to provide judgment-free guidance when you need it and can even remind you of your rules and expectations when you are on the edge of slipping up.

As we navigate this path and learn how to raise an explosive child like a pro, it is first important to deeply understand what explosive behavior is and the impact it has on the child, the parent, and the wider family, which is exactly what we are going to dive into in Chapter 1.

CHAPTER 1
UNDERSTANDING THE EXPLOSIVE CHILD

Clear is kind.

— BRENE BROWN

Many families across the world are grappling with the immense stress that often accompanies raising a child who is diagnosed with a disruptive behavioral disorder. Consider the following:

- 11% of children nationwide have received an ADHD diagnosis, with nearly two-thirds of them displaying at least one other mental, emotional, or behavioral disorder (Centers for Disease Control and Prevention, 2022; Danielson et al., 2018).
- 1 in 100 kids suffer from obsessive-compulsive disorder (OCD), often coupled with mood or anxiety disorders (Beyond OCD, 2018).

- Up to 16% of the childhood population contend with oppositional defiant disorder (ODD), marked by chronic hostility and volatility that strains family relationships (Whitbourne, 2003).

These startling statistics only just scratch the surface of the reality of raising a child with one of these conditions. The impact of explosive behavior stretches far beyond the child themselves; it can affect family relationships and self-esteem and can even impact parents' work and earnings if behavior is not manageable in traditional school settings. With compassion, education, and understanding, families *can* overcome these hurdles.

RECOGNIZING EXPLOSIVE BEHAVIOR AND ITS IMPACT

Children exhibiting explosive behavior display a certain set of behavioral and emotional patterns during what is sometimes termed "meltdowns." As touched on in the introduction, these are not your garden-variety tantrums that neurotypical children display when they are frustrated; these episodes involve prolonged and intense displays of anger, sadness, or frustration that often appear grossly disproportionate to the triggering situation (Mayo Clinic Staff, 2019b). These meltdowns do not necessarily stem from a desire to have a need or a want met, as with neurotypical children, but from sensory overload and overwhelm.

Let's now look in more detail at the specific behaviors and patterns seen in explosive children.

Characteristics of Explosive Behavior

Typical explosive outburst behaviors may include any of the following (Kaminski & Claussen, 2017; Parekh, 2017; Waller, 2015):

- Crying, screaming, or yelling for a lengthy period of time, potentially lasting over 20–30 minutes.
- Aggression toward others in the form of hitting, kicking, or pushing.
- Self-injury, such as head-banging, biting, or scratching oneself.
- Destruction of property by throwing, crushing, or ripping items.
- Refusing to move or follow directives despite parents' efforts to convince them.
- Risky, impulsive behaviors like running into traffic or self-harm threats.

These episodes can typically last far longer than is usual for a child's age and developmental stage, often ranging from 20 minutes to well over an hour. The triggers for these episodes do not always make sense to the parent or caregiver, sometimes stemming from a minor frustration and escalating into a full-blown meltdown. Parents and caregivers are often left at a loss for what to do as all attempts to redirect them or console them won't work.

The unpredictability around what triggers the child can be distressing for the parents, leaving them with the feeling of constantly "walking on eggshells" and looking for signs that an episode is on the horizon.

Another factor that separates an explosive episode from a typical tantrum is the sheer intensity of the outburst. With a tantrum, the trigger is usually fairly obvious to the parent or caregiver and, depending on the age of the child, is an age- and developmentally-appropriate response that can be understood and handled. An explosive child's meltdown may seemingly come from nowhere or stem from something that might appear inoffensive, like asking them to stop what they are doing to come and have dinner.

Understanding the Impact

Episodes of explosive outbursts are relentless, intense, and unpredictable. Because of this, they can have a huge impact on the child's emotional health and self-esteem. These children are not blind to their faults, especially as they grow older and more self-aware. They often experience a deep sense of shame after each episode and will often think back over past meltdowns when they are reminded of them, locking them in that cycle of shame. They are also likely to experience anxiety around their own behavior, wondering when the next episode is going to happen and dreading what the next trigger may be. The effect that this has on the child's self-esteem can be catastrophic. They cannot control their own reactions and may even begin to dislike themselves for that. They blame themselves for not being able to control their outbursts and being unable to verbalize what is going on.

The ripple effects on families can be equally as devastating. Parents find themselves constantly on edge, watching for even the smallest sign of another outburst. The dread and worry can cause them to turn down invitations and cancel plans because they worry about the unpredictability of the scenario they are taking their explosive child into. They may also be fueled by shame, not wanting to see the accusation on others' faces when their kiddo inevitably has yet another episode out in public. It can be extremely isolating to be a parent in this situation.

That's not to mention the resentment that parents may foster toward their child or the resentment that siblings may be carrying. They may also refuse to go out in public with their explosive brother or sister because they are embarrassed about the meltdown behavior.

At school, the child's behavior may be disrupting the learning of other students as well as themselves. They might even be destructive—at school and at home—and cause damage to school equipment. Teachers and schools are not always equipped with all the resources they need to manage this kind of behavior, so they, too, will end up walking on eggshells, trying their best to maintain order for the whole class and keep the explosive child calm.

You see, the effects of this behavior are not confined only to the child experiencing it. Disruption and destruction echo outward, causing chaos and anxiety to almost every person the child interacts with.

Debunking Myths

Research into these mental health conditions has been up and down for the last 50 years (Sonuga-Barke et al., 2022), which means there are some enduring, uneducated myths that are still prevalent in society, and it's important to debunk them here. These myths can be really damaging, and believing them may prevent parents from seeking the help they need for their children.

Myth: It's Just Bad Parenting

Fact: Research shows that genetics, brain chemistry, and neurodevelopmental factors—not parenting—determine these disorders. While parenting strategies can help manage behaviors, "teaching parenting skills does not markedly improve the symptoms of ADHD" (ADHD Awareness, 2019). Therefore, parents do not cause or exacerbate underlying clinical diagnoses.

Myth: The Kid Should Know Better

Fact: Due to developmental delays in areas like emotional regulation, impulse control, and decision-making, explosive children cannot inherently "know better." Their outbursts are not caused by a lack of education.

Myth: Punishment Is the Best Way to Correct Explosive Behavior

Fact: Evidence proves that positive reinforcement and teaching missing skills are far more effective in the long term than punishment. Punishment tends to further distress children during meltdowns (Kaminski et al., 2017). Explosive children do not need to be punished; they need compassionate support and guidance.

Myth: These Disorders Aren't "Real" Mental Health Conditions

Fact: ADHD, ODD, and OCD are all recognized globally by medical organizations as being legitimate mental health conditions, not only in children but also in adults across the world. In fact, there are even suggestions that people who have long since died potentially had these conditions; one of the greatest physicians of all time, Albert Einstein, is said to have had ADHD (ADHD Embrace, n.d.).

The truth is that the complexity and multifaceted nature of explosive behavior could not be caused or treated by any one thing, which is why we cannot simply blame bad parenting or use harsh punishment to "fix" our children. There are so many factors layered together in the child's neurological makeup that cannot be explained by one simple judgment. This is why maintaining realistic expectations while untangling the web of neurological complexity with our children is the only effective way of successfully dealing with explosive behavior.

IDENTIFYING THE SIGNS AND SYMPTOMS

The next step in understanding explosive behavior lies in identifying the signs and symptoms. This involves learning to recognize the early warning signs, understanding the role of developmental stages, and knowing when it's time to seek help from outside sources.

Early Warning Signs

Signs of an explosive disorder in a child begin before the age of 12 and can be spotted as young as 3 (Mayo Clinic Staff, 2019a). Below, you will find a list of the most common early warning signs to look out for. Although some of these may look like typical toddler or child behavior, you should also consider the cause of the behavior and whether the behavior matches the trigger:

- Prolonged tantrums exceeding 15 minutes.
- Destructive tendencies like breaking toys or hitting parents.
- Inability to regulate sadness, anger, or disappointment without adult intervention.
- Extreme emotional volatility.
- Violent rages at siblings over minor disputes.
- Sensory overreactions like loud shrieks to scratchy clothing.
- Absent or under-developed self-calming skills.

Spotting the signs of these disorders early can help ease the impact that it has, not only on the child but on the family as well. The sooner you get a diagnosis, the sooner you can begin taking measures to improve the situation, such as behavior therapy and teaching emotional regulation. Early intervention helps to strengthen skills and can sometimes prevent these concerning markers from spiraling into chronic behavior disorders (Early Intervention Foundation, 2018).

The Role of Developmental Stages

As children grow, the signs and symptoms of behavioral disorders will vary. This means that the way parents and caregivers approach and tackle explosive behavior will have to change as well. Understanding developmental timelines can help you to identify any issues and address them quickly.

The table below lists common neurotypical behaviors for the three major age groups vs. concerning explosive behaviors for easy reference.

Developmental stage	Neurotypical behaviors	Concerning "explosive" behaviors
Toddler (1–3)	• Short tantrums when frustrated • Limited self-soothing skills • Impulsive physical responses like biting	• Frequent tantrums exceeding 15+ minutes • Prolonged intense crying or screaming • Aggression toward parents (hitting, hair pulling) • Inability to self-regulate without adult help
Childhood (6–11)	• Beginning to master emotional reactions • Expanding communication skills • Testing rules and boundaries	• Verbal abuse or hurtful language • Impulsive defiance of rules • Physical aggression over minor triggers
Teens (12+)	• Maturing self-control • Conflicts resolved with words • Testing limits through rebellion	• Raging over insignificant problems • Risky or destructive behavior • Self-injury threats during meltdowns

Human beings are fluid, as are our emotions. We are all constantly changing, learning, and growing, and this is particularly true of behavior. Just because a child cannot master emotional regulation in middle childhood does not mean they are going to struggle in their teens or that behavior inevitably has to escalate. However, sometimes behavior does escalate beyond our capacity to cope with it and that is when you may need to seek external help.

When to Seek Help

Deciding when you and your child need professional support for their behavior can be extremely challenging.

While all kids have tantrums, explosive episodes signal underlying issues needing evaluation if (National Health Service, 2021, Yale Medicine, n.d.):

- They occur 3+ times per week, lasting over 15 minutes.
- Self-harm, violence toward others, or destruction of property occurs.
- Behavior severely impacts school performance and family functioning.
- Caregiver interventions consistently fail to de-escalate or comfort.
- Warning signs emerge prior to age 4.

If your child is experiencing frequent explosive episodes with these features, then it is time to seek professional help. Seeing your usual pediatrician is the first step, as they can then refer families to child psychologists, psychiatrists, therapists, and behavioral specialists who are equipped to accurately diagnose and treat conditions like ADHD, anxiety, OCD, and ODD.

The process begins with thorough interviews of parents and children about symptoms, family history, and timelines. They may also contact the school to get their input. There may be evaluations like behavior rating scales or IQ and neuropsychological testing (Fletcher, 2013). Based on the results, they will then offer a treatment plan which may involve medication, therapy, or perhaps even both. It is important to remember that this is a process of ongoing collaboration, and there will be adjustments over time to adapt to the child's changing needs.

Reputable resources to find licensed professionals and other support include:

- American Academy of Child and Adolescent Psychiatry: www.aacap.org
- Psychology Today's Therapist Finder: www.psychologytoday.com
- National Alliance on Mental Illness Helpline: 1-800-950-6264 or info@nami.org
- Children and Adults with Attention-Deficit/Hyperactivity Disorder (CHADD): chadd.org
- International OCD Foundation: iocdf.org

Getting an accurate diagnosis and building a strong support system around families and their children can mean the difference between struggling into adulthood and thriving.

COMMON TRIGGERS AND STRESSORS

Even though it may feel like episodes of explosive behavior come out of nowhere, the truth is they are always triggered by something, and there are always signs that your child's behavior is about to go downhill rapidly.

Identifying Triggers

Let's take a look at some of the most common triggers of explosive behavior, also known as the stimuli. According to Zauderer (2023), "The stimulus, sometimes called a circumstance, that begins a negative behavior reaction is called a trigger."

Triggers

This list is not exhaustive, and every child will have different triggers; these are just the most common (Achieve Beyond, 2021; Mayo Clinic Staff, 2022; Kaminski et al., 2017):

- Being denied access to preferred items or activities
- Transitions and changes in routine
- Rule changes or schedule disruptions
- Situations causing embarrassment or a perception of failure
- Feelings of loss of control, helplessness, boredom, or anger
- Overstimulating environments like loud noises or crowds
- Struggles with communication skills to express needs
- Unexpected touch, textures, smells, or visual stimuli
- Poor sleep, hunger, or diet issues

Precursors

One of the most useful tools in your parenting toolbox is catching the early warning signs that your child is about to have an episode and learning how to intervene or redirect that behavior. These subtle, early signs are known as *precursors*. By taking note of these signs, it is possible to catch the episode before the child becomes too emotionally dysregulated. You will be able to see that an explosion is coming, and you can completely change the course of the episode and maybe even prevent it from happening using tools such as distraction, emotional support, or removal from the trigger.

Some of the more common precursors include (LEARN Behavioral, 2019):

- Clenched fists, tensed shoulders, or pacing that may signal mounting internal tension.
- Subtle signs of irritation like eye rolling, under-breath muttering, or foot tapping.
- Yawning, seeking isolation, or self-soothing behaviors like hair twirling also tend to surface.
- Verbal precursors can include grunting, whining, or challenging statements like "This is stupid!" or "You're mean!"

These precursors indicate the child is very close to losing emotional control. If you can train yourself to notice these signs, you will have the opportunity to ask what's wrong, validate feelings, suggest a break, or remove the child from the triggering situation. The key is to use empathy and action to divert the potential meltdown.

The ABC Model

Here, it is also appropriate to discuss the ABC model to help you understand why behavior happens (FSA, 2015).

Antecedent: This refers to the stimulus or trigger preceding a behavior. As explained above, this can be anything in the environment that impacts the child's senses and serves as a trigger for the subsequent behavior. Some common antecedents include transitions, disruption of routines, sensory discomfort, criticism, and so on.

Behavior: This is the observable action displayed by the child in response to the antecedent or stimulus. Think back to the list of common explosive behavioral reactions—tantrums, crying, yelling, aggression, property destruction, and non-compliance with directives. The behavior directly follows and is evoked by whatever stimulus event preceded it.

Consequence: The consequence refers to what happens directly after the behavior occurs. This consequence can reinforce either positive or negative behaviors, increasing or decreasing the likelihood of the behavior recurring. Examples of consequences include praise, attention, being given a preferred item or activity, or even removal from an undesirable situation. Punitive consequences like criticism, withholding privileges, or the absence of praise may reinforce undesired behaviors as well.

Analyzing the connections using this Antecedent-Behavior-Consequence sequence will help parents as they try to uncover the patterns that lead to explosive behavior and replace problematic reinforcers, encouraging positive behavioral responses instead.

Documenting and Analyzing Behavior

Educating yourself about what your child's triggers are and what kinds of precursor behavior they display is the most important step as you begin this journey. Keep a journal and write everything down until you begin to see a pattern of behavior. Here are some of the things you should be keeping a note of to help you in your investigation:

- Date and time
- Duration
- Precursors observed
- Perceived triggers
- Location and people present
- Child's verbalizations and actions
- Caregiver response
- What calmed the child

This will be difficult at first; you will find yourself making a notation of every time your child has a meltdown and then you will have to try to remember if you noticed any precursor behavior and what the trigger was. You might realize that you did notice your child was tapping their foot before the episode. Over time, you will become more adept at noticing these things *before* the episode occurs, and your notes will become richer and full of useful data for you to work with.

Case Study

Allison almost reached her limit with her son Harley's explosive episodes when she had to carry him out of the school Christmas carol concert. Through tears, she latched onto one suggestion from Harley's teacher to try and track his triggers.

Over the next few weeks, she kept a written log of all of Harley's meltdowns. It all felt a bit depressing to start with, as she had a long list of episodes and no other data. She soon started noticing and remembering other key details and jotting them down, too. She noticed that Harley would regularly hit himself in the head around his ears and started to watch out for other signs that loud noises could be the problem.

Using her notes and observations, Allison was able to determine that loud, sudden noises were a huge trigger for Harley and got him some ear defenders. The following year, Harley sat happily through the whole Christmas carol concert with his ear defenders on, tapping his feet along to the music.

Environmental and Emotional Stressors

Both the internal and external landscape can influence the behavior regulation of all children, not just those with ODD, ADHD, and OCD. Think about the way a child light up when they see the playground in the distance and how they dart off into the sea of children and equipment. The exciting location influences their emotional landscape, bringing them joy and excitement. The issue arises when a child with these conditions finds themselves in an environment that is overstimulating or distressing for them. In this case, they are more likely to have an explosive outburst because of their limited coping capacity. Playgrounds may even be their trigger —these aren't necessarily places full of joy for all children.

Other settings that might be a trigger for explosive children include anywhere that is chaotic or noisy by its nature: shopping malls, classrooms, or family gatherings. It's really important to prepare children in advance if you are going to be taking them into an environment that is likely to trigger them. Let them know where you are going and give them more than one warning that the environment is about to change to help them prepare and adjust.

The same is true at home if they need to stop doing something fun and move on to something less fun—like getting ready for school. Give your child a thirty-minute warning to let them know that they will have to stop playing and get their shoes on. Remind them again fifteen minutes before they have to stop and again five minutes before. As we have learned, these children can really struggle with transition, so it's important not to rush or interrupt them. If you can help it. Small adjustments like this can really change the reaction and make the whole process of transitioning smoother.

Emotionally, explosive children struggle with accurately identifying their own internal states. You see, part of the problem is their lack of or limited emotional awareness, and this prevents them from being able to articulate deeper feelings. If you ask them what's wrong, they are more than likely just going to tell you that they are feeling "upset," with no clear reasoning or understanding behind that feeling—explosive reactions are the substitute for words.

Creating a Trigger-Free Environment

We have defined what explosive behavior is, what it looks like, and how it manifests. We looked at the triggers and stimuli behind the behavior and discussed the signs and precursors that we might notice before the behavior escalates. Let's close this chapter by now looking at different strategies and practical tips for creating a trigger-free environment. With our children's well-being in mind, we can make small (and sometimes large) adjustments that help to prevent explosive episodes and bring a semblance of calm to our chaotic lives.

Creating a Supportive Low-Stress Environment

Preparation, preparation, preparation. That's really all there is to it. Reducing triggers simply means getting ahead of them. Now that you have spent some time tracking them, you should have a better understanding of what your child's triggers are, and now you can start to mitigate them.

To help you, here is a list of some of the more common actions you can take to get ahead of the explosions and create a trigger-free environment (CDC, 2006; Kaminski & Claussen, 2017; National Health Service England, 2022):

Reduce external stimuli:

- Stick to set routines so the child knows what to expect.
- Give your child warnings before transitioning to new activities or locations.
- Play calming background music and use soft lighting.
- Keep shared family spaces tidy and minimize clutter.

Promoting predictability:

- Post visual daily schedules for structured consistency.
- Discuss any changes to plans or exceptions to routine ahead of time.
- Set timers or alerts so your child can anticipate activity endings.

Using clear communication:

- Give concise, age-appropriate directives focused on positive actions.
- Allow extra time for following instructions.
- Check for comprehension by having your child repeat key steps.
- Provide frequent, supportive feedback on progress.

As parenting expert Brene Brown (n.d.) wisely states, "Clear is kind, unclear is unkind." Having set routines, fostering predictability, and having clear communication with your child are so important in minimizing triggers and explosive behavior. These steps are going to help you set your child up for success instead of failure.

We don't expect a newborn baby to get up and walk the day they are born; the baby has to build their muscles up from nothing. It takes anywhere from 10 months to 2 years for a baby to become strong enough to take those first steps, and in the meantime, we make adjustments. We carry them from place to place, we play with them to help them build those core muscles, and we nurture them through growth. Making adjustments for your explosive child is the same in many ways; you are allowing them the space to be at ease, where they can play without anxiety, and build their emotional muscles that will eventually allow them to combat their explosive behavior.

CHAPTER 2

THE UNDERLYING CAUSES

Parents who speak with their children about their feelings have children who develop emotional intelligence and can understand their own and other people's feelings more fully.

— DANIEL J. SIEGEL

School mornings had become something of a war zone for Roger and Nikki. The problem? Asking their daughter, Hayley, to get dressed and ready for school. At seven years old, Roger and Nikki could not understand why this simple task could cause such an eruption. Hayley was known to rage and scream for up to 45 minutes when they tried to ask her to put her school clothes on.

Roger and Nikki tried everything they could think of. They remained as calm and patient as possible and asked her gently; they gave her plenty of warnings leading up to the moment she had to get dressed; they tried punishing her, convincing her, and pleading with her. They would lay her clothes out in a neat pile every morning so she wouldn't feel overwhelmed trying to find all the different items in her wardrobe. They tried getting her dressed as soon as she woke up in the morning, and they tried leaving it to the very last minute before leaving for school. Nothing worked.

Eventually, they decided Hayley must be grappling with oppositional defiance disorder or a related condition, and they approached the school for help. One morning, while observing her for her evaluation, Hayley's teacher noticed how often she picked and scratched at her shirt. When she asked Hayley if her shirt felt uncomfortable, Hayley replied that it "felt like fire."

Hayley's teacher had uncovered the underlying reason behind the explosive mornings. It transpired that the sensory discomfort of her shirt was coupled with the unpredictability of her mornings as her parents desperately tried different things to help her get dressed without a meltdown. Due to her lack of emotional regulation skills, Hayley was responding to her sensory overload and panic every morning in the only way that she knew how—explosive outbursts.

This breakthrough insight from her teacher finally shifted the narrative for Hayley and her parents—her brain was sending inaccurate danger signals, and her behavior was not intentional rebellion.

Roger, Nikki, and Hayley were able to work with an occupational therapist, where they uncovered the clothing textures that Hayley could tolerate. They were able to tailor her wardrobe with shirts that were comfortable for her so that dressing no longer induced unbearable hypersensitivity. They were also able to establish a consistent morning routine, which no longer triggered Hayley's panic. School mornings were completely transformed.

Here, the issues lay in communication barriers and sensory/emotional issues. Once these were addressed compassionately, Hayley's parents watched morning battles dissolve into harmony. Their explosive child was finally met with empathy instead of punishment, granting her the space that she so desperately needed to grow and be calm.

In this chapter, we are going to consider the role of emotional dysregulation, communication barriers, and neurodevelopmental considerations as underlying causes of explosive behavior in children.

EMOTIONAL REGULATION CHALLENGES

Emotional regulation refers to how we manage our emotions in response to thoughts, feelings, and external situations. We all experience emotions like happiness, sadness, and anger, but our responses vary based on individual differences. Emotion regulation involves developing skills over time to react to emotional triggers with appropriate levels of response—skills that some individuals struggle with more than others (National Health Service, n.d.).

It's a skill that most of us will learn in childhood and develop as we move into adulthood. Because they have yet to master this skill, children often rely on caregiver support to co-regulate big emotions, requiring parents to be aware of their own reactions. As parents, we are constantly modeling behavior for our children, and because of this, parental regulation is key.

Even as children grow older, they may still need extra support regulating emotions during difficult times. In essence, emotion regulation entails handling one's feelings with self-control and flexibility —abilities requiring continual nurturing.

But what happens when adults and children have challenges with emotional regulation?

Defining Emotional Dysregulation

According to the Cleveland Clinic (2023), emotional dysregulation refers to having "trouble controlling your emotions and how you act on those feelings." In explosive children, emotional dysregulation refers to an inability to manage emotional responses to frustrations, transitions, disappointments, or even positive events and can manifest as inappropriate emotional reactions where the intensity, frequency, and duration of feelings seem disproportional to the trigger. This means that, for our explosive children, minor triggers rapidly escalate into extreme emotional and behavioral reactions.

When we have emotional regulation skills, we are able to manage our feelings and reactions to things. We can verbalize our needs or distract ourselves from the things that make us feel overwhelmed. Picture emotional regulation as having control of a switch, similar to the volume control on your phone. Someone with good emotional regulation skills will be able to turn that switch up and down using healthy coping skills they have learned. Children with emotional dysregulation have no control over this switch and, many times, don't even realize it exists. They lack the control skills that typically strengthen with maturity, so emotions and outbursts escalate quickly.

This kind of dysregulation renders children helpless against the kinds of outbursts we have already discussed. They might appear to have the emotional coping skills of a toddler at the age of eight when such meltdowns should really be behind them.

Dysregulated children lack the skills to

- Self-soothe
- Distract from distress
- Communicate needs verbally.

As discussed, emotional regulation skills typically develop gradually as children mature both cognitively and socially. Different emotional coping strategies will develop at different developmental stages, such as impulse control, delay of gratification, reading social cues, and communicating needs verbally (Wesarg-Menzel et al., 2023).

It's important to note that environmental factors also play a crucial role in the development of emotional regulation. Behavior displayed by their parents and caregivers can also be supportive or detrimental to children, solidifying these skills depending on how successful the caregiver is at regulating their own emotions (Gottman et al., 1996). Remember, children model and mirror the behavior that they see and experience from others. If parents consistently display emotional dysregulation, children are more likely to display these behaviors as well. Neglect or trauma can also severely hinder the development of self-regulation capacity (Dvir et al., 2014).

Other factors must also be considered here. Psychiatric conditions, neurological differences, or trauma exposure can disrupt the maturation of both the brain systems and environmental supports underpinning emotional regulation (Sherin & Nemeroff, 2011).

Learning regulation tactics is essential to overcoming the volatile and exaggerated emotional episodes that can occur due to emotional dysregulation. But before we can help our children overcome this hurdle, we must first recognize the signs.

Case Study

At the age of eight, Amber struggled with her emotional regulation. She would often go from zero to ten in an instant when she felt frustrated or disappointed. When playing board games with her siblings, she would demand to be in control of tasks like rolling the dice or using the spinner. Her parents encouraged fair turn-taking during play, but Amber's frustration would boil up when her siblings took their turn.

One day, during a game of twister, Amber demanded to be the only one to spin the spinner despite her brother also asking to have a turn. She snatched the spinner away from her brother and shrieked that he wasn't allowed. Her parents decided to stop the game because the fun had stopped. This only escalated Amber's episode, and soon, they were trying to manage a full-blown meltdown of screaming and kicking.

Recognizing the Signs

Now that we know what emotional dysregulation is, it's time to take a look at how it presents itself. Here are some of the clues that a child might be struggling (Elliott, n.d.; Kearney, 2021)

- Frequent intense tantrums exceeding 15–20 minutes involving kicking, screaming, and self-harm threats.
- Destructive behaviors like throwing toys, ripping artwork off walls, and breaking possessions.
- Verbal abuse of parents or teachers, including aggressive yelling and hateful statements.
- Inability to move on from minor disappointments, becoming inconsolably upset.
- Limited range of emotional expression—generally just anger or sadness.

These signs might present differently across different settings. At home, a lack of emotional regulation tends to surround ordinary incidents like sibling quarrels or turning off screens. Emotionally overloaded kids cannot articulate their distress and instead react explosively in the only way they know how. They also cannot self-soothe or gain control of themselves without adult intervention once the episode has escalated.

School settings present further challenges, with changes in routine, social interactions, and performance expectations all sparking big feelings that a dysregulated child cannot manage alone. Meltdowns often leak into classroom spaces, amplifying the distress and later triggering feelings of shame and unworthiness.

Strategies for Parents of Emotionally Dysregulated Children

The next question we must ask is what are parents supposed to do when they notice the signs of dysregulation? Here are some hands-on, actionable tips to help parents in the moment (O'Neal et al., 2019):

- Validate struggles by labeling big emotions. You can use phrases like: "You seem very upset right now." Name specific feelings like anger or sadness if possible: "I see you are feeling angry that you can't have more cookies."
- Coach calming strategies like deep belly breaths, visualization of a peaceful place, or progressive muscle relaxation. It's best to have these discussions and introduce these skills during calm moments, as your child is in no position to learn new skills during an episode. It's also extremely important to model self-soothing techniques alongside the child in distress—do the deep breathing with them and coach them through it.
- Consider sensory supports like noise-canceling headphones, weighted blankets, or fidget toys during situations involving lots of stimulation. You should also be proactive and remove the child from overstimulating environments as needed.

- Communicate empathy and care through both words and a caring touch when possible. Physical touch can help to ground your child and will help to reassure them that they are safe and loved even through big reactions.
- Allow space for physical outlets like screaming into pillows or ripping paper when needed so feelings don't lead to destructive meltdowns. Keep in mind to set appropriate boundaries regarding space and property: "You are not allowed to throw your sister's toys, but you can tear up this paper."
- Offer structured outlets like drawing emotions or role-playing scenarios with stuffed animals that allow processing big feelings in constructive ways.
- Take care to avoid further escalating reactions through criticism, threats of punishment, or angry tones, which can perpetuate the intensity. Respond gently and without judgment. It's important to remind yourself that your child is not trying to manipulate or control you, and you don't have to respond in kind—children are not evil masterminds with ulterior motives. Explosions are beyond the realm of their control.

The key is validating a dysregulated child's experience while also consistently nurturing the development of self-regulation skills over time through modeling, practice, and compassion. What matters most is communicating to them your unconditional support. Don't just say it; show it.

Impact on Behavior and Family Dynamics

When children lack skills regulating emotions, even minor frustrations can rapidly snowball into explosive meltdowns due to an overwhelmed nervous system and adrenaline spikes. They may be triggered by things like denied requests or boredom, which can create internal turmoil that their normal coping abilities cannot contain. This emotional overload manifests into exaggerated external behaviors—raging, hitting, destructive tantrums—reflecting profound inner distress kids cannot articulate or control.

For families, the relentless uncertainty and chaos surrounding a dysregulated child leave all members in constant survival mode, unsure when the next detonation will erupt or how bad the fallout will spread. Parents cannot relax knowing that at any moment, a minor disruption like ending screen time could set off a 45-minute full-blown explosion, dragging the entire household into a state of high alarm. Everyone begins to live in a state of perpetual waiting, constantly expecting the next meltdown and trying to tiptoe around the child.

Sibling resentment simmers as the explosive child demands excessive time and attention, disrupting family outings or activities. Marital stress compounds the tension as exhausted parents snap at each other, disagreeing over disciplinary approaches while unable to find the time or the emotional energy to nurture intimacy. Though unintended, the dysregulated child monopolizes the family's emotional resources by continuously having to defuse or endure regular episodes that seemingly cannot be prevented or eased. For already vulnerable families, the damage to relationships and home life further entrenches the child's distress and blowups in a vicious cycle.

Narratives From Struggling Families:

"George has a heart of gold. He's so loyal and helpful—always sticking up for other kids at school. But he's not very good at making friends. High school has been a huge transition for him. He's having episodes almost daily, and the other kids don't know what to make of him."

"Oh-my-goodness, it's hard! Having her diagnosis now helps us to understand *why* she has these meltdowns, but we still aren't any closer to overcoming them. Alice is so upset with herself afterward. We're hoping to start behavioral therapy in the new year, and we have some parenting classes lined up."

COMMUNICATION BARRIERS

Next, we must consider the role of communication in causing or leading to escalated situations.

A major contributor to explosive behavior involves communication barriers between parents and children. Kids lacking emotional awareness or the vocabulary to articulate their distress often depend on their parents and caregivers to help them label and work through their big feelings (Gottman et al., 1996). However, busy or flustered parents often miss the subtle cues that signal rising turmoil in children.

Identifying Communication Breakdowns

Children don't just have explosive behaviors; these behaviors are often modeled for them. If the parents want the behavior to be fixed, they should not blame or shame the child. They have to model what they would like, and they have to make sure that their own emotions are regulated throughout the explosive behavior, which is often easier said than done.

A child showing early signs of frustration when an activity ends may exhibit subtle cues like fidgeting or grunting. Yet parents who are determined to stay in "control" of the situation may continue to sternly order cleanup while ignoring these precursors, warning them that the frustration is likely going to erupt into an episode. Without adequate mirroring and validation, kids' emotions will escalate unchecked (Pietro, 2016). Offlineing to both verbal and physical signals allows parents to intervene by acknowledging and normalizing fears or disappointment before they can escalate into explosions. Taking a pause to ask the child, "What's going on?" and then listening intently will defuse rather than fuel the big emotions. It's very important to confirm that it's all right to feel upset or scared, as this reassures kids that their feelings are heard even if their requests can't always be granted. Validating your child while also setting limits and boundaries prevents emotions from mounting to explosive proportions.

Alternative Communication Strategies

There are many alternative communication strategies that parents can learn and implement to improve exchanges and understanding with emotionally overloaded kids at risk of explosions. Let's explore a few now.

To start, simplifying language to be more concrete while naming specific feelings proves to be hugely beneficial (Murray, 2014). For instance, telling children to "calm down" or "behave" fails to communicate behavioral expectations—these kinds of instructions are extremely vague and do not offer anything constructive to do instead. Whereas "use gentle hands with your sister" or "speak softly to me" provides them with further clarity needed to adjust their behavior and tells them what *to* do instead of what *not* to.

It can also be really helpful to use an observation like, "Your fists are clenched; what seems to be the matter?" coupled with a physical touch—place your hand soothingly on their arm or shoulder. This helps children to connect internal feelings to external signals that they would not have noticed otherwise.

It is absolutely critical to identify and label the emotions a child is feeling with them. According to Siegel and Bryson (2011), when children become overwhelmed by big emotions like anger, fear, or sadness, the reasoning and thinking brain goes "offline" as the emotional brain takes over. Behaviorally, this looks like tantrums, yelling, or crying meltdowns.

Verbalizing the emotions the child seems to be experiencing—"You look really sad right now"—activates the thinking brain, enabling it to come back online and make sense of the situation. Putting feelings into words engages the intellectual part of the mind, lowering the intensity of the emotional hijack. It's as if you are shining a flashlight on the monster in a dark room, and it makes it seem less scary. Simply saying, "I see you feel very angry," starts to deflate the emotional overload. After naming the feeling, parents can then talk through more constructive solutions once the child feels soothed enough to listen and reflect.

Pay attention to their body language; look for signs like furrowed brows or aggressive gestures because this will let you know that they need verbal support. In fact, think about pre-verbal children for a moment here, who rely exclusively on non-verbal communication. Pre-verbal and nonverbal children need emotional mirroring through facial expressions, tone of voice, and safe physical contact to feel soothed when spiraling because they don't have the capacity to use words (Gottman et al., 1996).

These alternative approaches enable the emotional stabilization required for avoiding catastrophic explosive episodes through mutually understood communication for both the child and the parent.

Exercise: Emotionally Connect THEN Redirect

Here is a handy exercise you can try out with your child the next time they are experiencing a big emotion. Pay attention to how this technique shifts the dynamic and changes the outcome of the episode.

Goal: Manage meltdowns through connection and redirection.

When a child shows early signs of distress, such as crying or agitation (Siegel & Bryson, 2011):

- Move close to the child and gently make physical contact through a hand on the shoulder or arm around their back if appropriate. Make eye contact.
- Use a soft, calm tone to describe what is happening and validate their feelings—"I see you are getting very upset because it's time to leave the playground."
- Demonstrate that you hear through nods and facial expressions like raised eyebrows. Say supportive statements like, "It's disappointing to stop playing; I understand."
- Once the initial intensity lessens, suggest solutions or directives, still with empathy. For example, "I get how hard this transition is right now. Let's take three deep breaths together first. Then, we can walk together."

The priority is first connecting through compassionate words, tone, and safe touch so the child feels truly felt before problem-solving solutions. This lays the groundwork for receptivity instructions meant to redirect behavior.

Case Study

Arthur didn't believe it was going to work at first. He was raised with punishment and control and couldn't understand how empathy and communication could be more effective. His wife Anita convinced him to give it a try and gave him the ADHD resources from the pediatrician to read through.

Much to Arthur's surprise, when he stopped demanding that his son do as he was told and started asking him why he was having trouble with it, the meltdowns started to give way to fragile conversations about the boy's internal struggles. Arthur realized that his son needed to do things slightly differently. He discovered a more intimate side to parenting and, in doing so, was able to help his family navigate the ADHD diagnosis with significantly fewer outbursts.

Building a Two-Way Communication Channel

Being able to set limits and express empathy is extremely important in the communication process; it lays the groundwork to allow you to establish an open dialogue with the child. They will feel safe and comfortable to articulate any worries or problems that they have. When you can provide this safe space to contain their big feelings, emotions, and worries, you are helping them to find their voice, and this will help dramatically with their emotional regulation over time.

Let's look at some practical ways in which you can create a healthy two-way communication channel with your child (NSPCC, 2022; Young Minds, n.d.-a):

- You could create a designated space where you have one-on-one conversations with your child. This space should be comfortable and calming for the child, where you can talk about anything, including big feelings, although you shouldn't attempt to use this space to talk during an episode.
- Show your child that they have your attention; make eye contact and use active listening skills to show them that you are engaged in what they are saying. Set aside your phone or any other distractions and show them with your body language that you are listening.
- Reflect their emotions and what they are saying back at them to show them verbally that you are listening. If your child tells you they cried at school today, you could say, "It sounds like you were sad at school today."

- Another proactive way of opening up communication and helping them to identify personal coping strategies is by asking them what they need when you notice them starting to show signs of a meltdown.

Although a lack of communication can contribute to explosive behavior, by encouraging and building effective communication with your child, you can help them to learn some necessary skills for emotional regulation.

NEURODEVELOPMENTAL CONSIDERATIONS

Having looked at emotional regulation and communication challenges, let's now turn to consider how neurodiversity can contribute to explosive behavior.

Understanding Neurodiversity

Neurodevelopmental conditions like ADHD, OCD, ODD, and autism spectrum disorder (ASD) all involve differences in how the brain develops and functions. As the Cleveland Clinic explains, these all represent divergences from "expected" neural development, together falling under the umbrella of *neurodiversity* (Cleveland Clinic, 2023b; Cleveland Clinic, 2023c).

Neurodiversity does not mean that there is something wrong with the individual who has the condition; instead, these conditions simply mean the brain operates differently from the "norm" and has its own strengths and challenges. Children with one or more of these conditions simply process stimuli and emotions differently from other children, and this often results in them struggling with regulation skills (Cleveland Clinic, 2023c). Things like transitions, uncertainty, sensory input, or disappointments would typically only trigger minor frustration in neurotypical kids. However, for neurodiverse children lacking coping outlets, these same events may trigger systemic emotional overload.

Let's think back to Hayley, our case study at the opening of the chapter. She was experiencing explosive behavior linked to both the sensory overload of the material of her shirt and the panic that was triggered by the lack of morning routine. Instead of ODD, as her parents initially suspected, Hayley was diagnosed with ASD and ADHD. Each of these conditions contributed to her episodes, and once they were understood and managed, she was able to find her equilibrium in the mornings.

Tailoring Approaches to Individual Needs

Let's be clear right off the bat: There is no one-size-fits-all approach to managing neurodevelopmental disorders. They are measured on a wide spectrum, which means that children require personalized support that meets them where they are, not where you think they should be.

Let's look at two different children, aged eight, who were diagnosed with ASD: Liam and Kiri.

Liam is considered "high functioning." He is at home in the class-room and excels at math, science, and art. He struggled with social communication; he consistently interrupts others and his blunt and honest nature has been known to cause upset and social awkwardness.

Kiri, on the other hand, presents as a more severe case of the condition. She is nonverbal and uses limited sign language and visual cues to communicate her basic needs. Kiri needs assistance with things like getting dressed and using the bathroom.

The parents of these children have their own tailored strategies for dealing with their disorder. Liam's parents focus on teaching him conversational rules like putting his hand up in class before he speaks, waiting patiently instead of interrupting, and ways to foster friendships. Kiri's parents focus on teaching visual cues and schedules; they teach Kiri how to indicate her needs using picture cards or using American Sign Language (ASL).

Both sets of parents respect their child's unique needs and tailor not only their strategies but also their expectations to the needs of their children.

Seeking Professional Support

Sometimes, personalized parenting and strategies just aren't enough to help manage the day-to-day challenges of these conditions. This is where the role of professionals comes in. Professional support can educate and equip families with additional resources to nurture their children.

There are different kinds of professionals who can assist when parents feel that the behavior their children are displaying goes beyond anything that they have the skills to cope with. It's best to seek help if you feel desperate or unequipped or if explosions are beginning to escalate in frequency and intensity despite implementing all the coping strategies in the explosive parenting toolkit.

Let's take a look at some of the professionals you might need and their roles (Mayo Clinic Staff, 2018; National Autistic Society, n.d.):

Psychologists

- Conduct cognitive, behavioral, and psychological evaluations to diagnose conditions.
- Provide individual and family therapy addressing behavioral challenges
- Teach regulation coping strategies and social communication skills

- Help manage emotional distress or co-occurring mental health issues

Psychiatrists

- Diagnose neurological and psychiatric conditions
- Prescribe and manage medications to improve focus, calm, and mood regulation.
- Monitor medication effectiveness and side effects

Educational specialists

- Evaluate academic, motor, speech, and functional performance
- Develop Individualized Education Programs (IEPs) outlining classroom accommodations
- Recommend remedial tutoring, speech therapy, physical therapy interventions
- Coordinate school-based services and progress monitoring

Occupational therapists

- Evaluate sensory processing and regulation difficulties
- Recommend sensory tools like weighted blankets, fidgets, noise-cancelling headphones
- Teach social skills and emotional identification vocabulary
- Guide adapting daily living routines for independent functioning

When you have these professionals involved in the care and development of your child, they will all collaborate with you and each other. They become a part of the "village," contributing to the care and well-being of your child.

Here, we've considered the role of emotional dysregulation, communication barriers, and neurodevelopmental conditions in explosive behaviors as some underlying causes. By now, you know that understanding the underlying causes is pivotal, and it is this understanding that lays the foundation for effective parenting strategies and skills.

CHAPTER 3

PARENTING STRATEGIES AND SKILLS

Offering a glimpse into the challenges of fatherhood, an anonymous dad shares:

I used to think that being a good parent meant being 'respected.' When I was a kid, we were supposed to be seen and not heard; we stayed quiet and out of the way, and if we broke the rules, we were punished. These days, we aren't allowed to hit kids, so when my son regularly screamed and attacked his sister over nothing, I would try to get him to listen and 'respect' me in the only other way I knew how—raising my voice and punishing him. The problem was that he just started screaming louder; it was like we were having a shouting match. The school introduced me to a bunch of resources—books and websites. We spoke to some specialists. I learned some hard truths; although my parenting didn't cause my son's behavior in the first place, it sure wasn't helping him. I was doubtful at first, but we started implementing the different parenting strategies we had learned. It took some time and a lot of patience that I didn't know I had, but eventually, my son stopped attacking and screaming at his sister. He still has outbursts now and then, and we help him to regulate his emotions as best we can. But his sister isn't afraid of him anymore, and our bond as a family feels like it's finally coming together.

Unfortunately, this is a common story. But thanks to this dad's honesty and openness to learning a new way, this family is going to break their generational cycle of damaging parenting practices. Now, it's important to reiterate here that explosive behavior is *NOT* caused by poor parenting. As we learned earlier when we were debunking the myths surrounding explosive behavior, things like genetics, brain chemistry, and neurodevelopmental factors each contribute to your child's outbursts (ADHD Awareness, 2019).

However...

As the dad above discovered, his outdated parenting practices were actually making the explosive episodes worse instead of better. We can all learn new strategies and skills that will not only improve our parenting but will expand our relationships with our children and help us as we guide them through their explosive nature.

COMMON PARENTING MISTAKES TO AVOID

Let's begin this chapter by first outlining the common mistakes parents make that we need to notice and avoid if we want to make any forward progress for ourselves and for our children. If you notice yourself in any of the behaviors listed below, please don't assume you are a terrible parent. You are here and you are willing to make that change—remember: When we *know* better, we *do* better. In the sections that follow this one, we will learn exactly how to do better.

Inconsistent Discipline

Research has demonstrated clear links between unpredictable discipline and child behavioral issues (Stormshak et al., 2000). Inconsistent discipline typically means that parenting fluctuates between being overly strict and then not following through. This does, unfortunately, have a significant effect on children's behavior.

Here are some examples of inconsistent discipline practices that could contribute to children's behavioral challenges:

- **Not following through on stated consequences:** Telling a child they will lose TV privileges if they don't finish homework, then allowing TV time anyway when they don't comply.
- **Uneven rule enforcement:** Punishing a child for having candy before dinner one night, then overlooking the infraction the next night.
- **Frequent threats without actions:** Warning a child you will take away their toy if they throw it again, but never actually confiscating it when they continue throwing.
- **Allowing tantrums and negotiating to sometimes "get your way":** Giving a child extra screen time after a tantrum, teaching them drama pays off occasionally.
- **Weekday vs weekend discrepancy:** Earlier bedtimes with no arguments during the week morph to flexible, later weekend bedtimes.
- **Mood-based responses:** Yelling at a child for spilling milk one day when you're already stressed versus calmly cleaning it up another day without reaction.
- **Role vs situation rigidity/flexibility:** Expecting formal, polite language from children with guests around but tolerating sarcasm when alone.

A longitudinal New Zealand study reveals "inconsistency was associated with early behaviour problems" in children by age nine, while strictness alone showed no correlation (Feehan et al., 1991). Unpredictability teaches kids that pushback or tantrums may result in parents abruptly caving to demands, which does nothing but incentivize them to repeatedly test boundaries and have meltdowns.

The problem with inconsistent discipline is that it appears random to the child—they don't have any insight into your inner workings and don't understand that being stressed from work makes you shout at them one day and respond calmly the next. We all understand the importance of routine for children—it's one of the first things we're taught to implement with our newborns—yet we often fail to see the connection between consistent parenting and consistent emotional responses from our children. If our response is unpredictable to the child, this can trigger stress and anxiety within them, leading them to "decrease their trust" (Pelini, 2023), and this then contributes to behavioral concerns. Kids thrive on stability and reliability—in *all* aspects of their lives.

The key to constructive discipline, as opposed to inconsistent discipline, lies in the following:

- **Make rules and stick to them:** Discussing family rules and writing them down with your child can incentivize you to be consistent with them. You could pin the family rules to the fridge so you can all return to them during periods of high emotion. Make sure the rules are fair for everyone.
- **Consequences for boundary-crossing:** This doesn't mean you have to shout at or punish your child. Aim for natural consequences that make sense to the child. For example, taking their iPads away because they had a meltdown at school won't benefit anyone because the "punishment" comes hours after the act and is unrelated.

This will only result in resentment and chip away at the parent–child relationship. If your child won't attempt to do their homework, then the natural consequence is that they don't get their screen time, which was planned for immediately after homework. If they are using a toy dangerously, then that toy will need to be removed for safety reasons. Taking a toy away because they won't eat their broccoli, on the other hand, does not make sense to them.

- **Privileges should be tied to responsibilities:** We'll discuss positive reinforcement more in-depth later in the chapter, but for now, consider the idea that things like iPads and screen time should not be an entitlement. Instead, it should be: "Well done! You completed your homework and you have earned an extra hour on the iPad." If you let them have the iPad regardless of whether they attempt their homework or not, then they will not feel incentivized to try.

The goal is to set clear expectations while communicating defined rewards and consequences. When this is done fairly, without bias, it builds accountability and trust, which leads to a stronger parent–child relationship and fewer meltdowns triggered by uncertainty.

Overlooking Emotional Needs

As we have discovered so far, explosive outbursts often happen when big feelings overwhelm a child's capacity to cope. Therefore, the first line of discipline should *not* be to overwhelm them even further by shouting, making demands, dishing out punishment, and seeking to take control.

Instead, it is important to connect, acknowledge and validate the emotions that they are feeling before expecting any kind of rational compliance from them. According to Thomas Sexton (2011), parents need to slow down, not blame or shame the child, and look at the situation from their point of view instead of ours. This means imagining oneself back in childhood when minor disruptions also felt significant in scale. When we rush to punish explosive behavior, we are only serving to further distress the child, whose nervous system is already under extreme pressure.

The other issue is when parents dismiss the emotional turmoil of the child and claim that it is simply attention-seeking and not real. The message that we send to our children when we tell them this is that *their feelings don't matter*. Instead of teaching them healthy coping mechanisms, we teach them to suppress big emotions simply because they are displeasing to others. This can have a catastrophic effect on mental well-being and will come back to haunt children in their teens and adulthood.

Over time, both of these reactions run the risk of magnifying the child's volatility while also eroding their self-esteem and trust in the support of their caregiver. Children who simply feel "too much" may come to see their intrinsic selves as somehow defective because the adults who are supposed to understand them implicitly cannot handle any of their big feelings. In the worst case scenarios, it can result in emotional deattatchment, dissassociative disorders, and mental health problems (Lindberg, 2007; Unity Point Health, n.d.).

Misinterpreting Behaviors

The final common parenting mistake that we are going to explore here is misinterpreting explosive behaviors. When we talked about overlooking emotional needs, I mentioned the idea that parents sometimes believe explosive behaviors are simply attention-seeking and not real. Well other misinterpretations include believing that the behavior is an attempt at manipulating their parents as an act of defiance. This kind of belief stems from the parent's lack of understanding of what is really going on in their child's mind and emotions.

Maladaptive behaviors can be described as actions that are not constructive coping responses and interfere with normal functioning (Conner, 2019). While adaptive aggression can serve defensive, competitive, or dominating ends productively, maladaptive aggression is inappropriate for situations and leads to individual or external distress—or, as we know it, explosive behavior. According to Sexton (2011), even defiant, maladaptive, and destructive behaviors serve an underlying purpose for the child driven by internal distress or unmet needs. This means that there is always an unmet need behind the behavior and it is never just defiance or manipulation. In other words, there is a noble intent behind the behavior that we must decode if we are to help the child deal with aggression.

Let's take a look at some examples of the noble intent behind the behavior and what that behavior might look like:

Noble intent	Example of behavior
Seeking attention or connection from inattentive or distracted parents—the child is trying to have any kind of interaction with the parent, even negative attention is better than no attention.	Ashley tries to show her parents that she learned how to do a cartwheel at school today. They barely look up from their work emails. Later on, she refuses to eat her dinner and the plate ends up on the floor.
Exerting control in response to powerlessness—when life feels unsafe or uncertain, the child seeks to take control over something.	Kai is being left out at school; the other children ditch him in the playground when he tries to play with them. At home, Kai is snappy and controlling when he plays with his younger sister. When she tries to add her own creativity to the game, Kai threatens her and gets angry.
Avoiding failure after repeatedly having difficulties socially or at school—avoiding the feelings of shame at all costs.	Taquira has fallen behind in math. She can't concentrate in class and the work looks like scribbles on the page. Instead of letting herself feel that shame, she becomes so disruptive in the classroom that she gets sent to the principal's office.
Numbing emotional pain—with little or no coping skills, it is easier to block out the pain than to sit with it.	William meets with his friends in the park after dark. One of them has brought a case of beer. After drinking one, William realizes he feels calmer and freer than ever. Drinking becomes a slippery slope for him.
Meeting sensory needs—these are often urgent and non-negotiable.	Ava hates the feeling of the seam of her sock when it moves across her toe. One morning, she and her mother are running late for school. Ava stops to adjust her sock three times on the way to school—which involves removing her shoe every time. Her mother gets stressed and angry, telling her to "get over it and walk; you'll forget about the sock soon." Ava can't simply forget about the discomfort and screams at her mother in the street.

The key here is learning how to identify the noble intent behind the behavior, which involves *reframing* the behavior. This can be extremely difficult to do in the moment, especially at first. When your own fight-or-flight reflex is triggered, much like your child, it can be tough to try and tap into your logical thinking and investigate the explosive behavior. Try asking yourself the following questions (Sexton, 2011):

- What is my child really feeling?
- How can I help them?

It can help to have an open and honest discussion with your child *after* the episode to see if they can give you any clues as to what the noble intent behind the behavior was. Once you have narrowed that down, you can then take steps to help them with their problem.

Let's look at Ava from above. When her mother, Sarah, got to work that day after dropping Ava at school, she sat down at her desk with her head in her hands and asked herself how she could make these stressful mornings easier for them both. She thought back over the morning, and the morning before that, and the morning before that. She realized that it was always the socks causing them to be late. The next morning, she counted how many times Ava removed her shoe and adjusted her sock: six times before they even left the house! As usual, Ava screamed and raged on the way to school. She waited until after school and discussed the socks with Ava. Ava told Sarah that when the sharp bit (the seam) slipped over her little toe, it made her want to scream and rip her own hair out.

Sarah went online and did a Google search for seam-free socks for kids. She ordered a couple of different brands to try. Over the next few weeks, Sarah was amazed to see how their morning routine shifted. Sometimes, the seam-free socks still bothered Ava, but nowhere near as often as before. They managed to make it to school on time and without rushing nearly every day from that point onward.

Because Sarah was able to stop and look for the noble intent behind Ava's meltdowns—her sensory needs—Sarah was able to help Ava avoid outbursts, and Sarah was better equipped to deal with them when they happened. She wouldn't get frustrated at Ava but instead allowed her the time she needed to remove her shoes and adjust her socks when she needed to, thus minimizing the outbursts as well.

FOUR ESSENTIAL SKILLS FOR MANAGING EXPLOSIVE BEHAVIOR

You'll be pleased to know that it's time for some practical, hands-on advice. In this section, we're going to look at the four essential skills for managing explosive behavior that are going to transform your parenting and your relationship with your child.

De-Escalation Techniques

Let's start with de-escalation techniques. These are probably the skills you are looking for right off the bat—how do we calm down explosive situations when it feels like episodes are inevitable?

First, look for the warning signs. Remember the precursors we discussed in Chapter 1; you should have an idea of what your child's specific warning signs are by now if you have been watching them carefully and taking note.

If you can de-escalate the situation before it erupts into a full-blown meltdown, you can prevent all the damage control often needed after an explosive episode.

Step-By-Step Guide for De-Escalation

1. **Speak calmly:** Make sure you are using a low, soft tone that models the calm that you are hoping to achieve in your child.

2. **Give them space:** It helps to get down to their eye level so you don't look intimidating, but be sure to give them ample physical space. Crowding an upset child is only going to make them feel even more overwhelmed.

3. **Offer empathy and emotional validation:** As previously mentioned, validation is key here. When the child feels seen and heard, you have access to connect, and then you can help them to regulate. You can say something like, "I know this is really hard right now. I'm here."

4. **Redirect them:** At this point, it can be helpful to redirect their attention to alternative activities. Think of something that provides them with sensory relief, like music, coloring, or play dough. You could take them away to a quiet space and away from the situation that triggered them.

5. **Provide a choice:** Remember, one of the noble intentions we discussed above was linked with control and powerlessness. If you offer the child a choice between two calming options, you are also giving them a greater sense of control.

Other De-Escalation Tips

- Another way to redirect frustration is to provide your child with fidget toys or stress balls. These can be particularly useful in the classroom or when your child is expected to sit still or concentrate for longer periods of time.
- Create a safe space for your child, somewhere they can go in the house when they feel safe or you see that an explosion is coming. You can make sure their favorite

blanket or toy is in the safe space for them to help soothe
them or have some fidget toys available there.

- If they have a tendency to get physically aggressive, then
  provide them with a physical outlet. Think of getting them
  a punching bag or letting them hit a pillow.
- Sometimes, music can be a great distraction. You could
  choose something calming, or if your child has a favorite
  song, make sure you always have it handy.
- Intentionally shift the mood. This can be tricky because
  you might not feel like being silly or playful when your
  child is on the edge of a meltdown, but silliness and
  playfulness can be mood-altering. Tell them a joke, sing
  them a song, or start dancing! This offers immediate
  connection, which may be what your child is seeking and is
  uplifting.

Narratives From Families

"Dancing has become my favorite de-escalating technique! When
Mikey comes to me in the kitchen with that face that says he's on
the edge, I turn up the radio, and we dance it out. Sometimes, he's
more resistant to it, but my silly moves always crack a smile from
him even if he doesn't join in. I can see the tension leaving his
body."

"Why did nobody tell me about validation while I was pregnant?
This should be in every parenting handbook! I admit, I used to huff
and roll my eyes, thinking, *What now?* But now, I squat down next
to AJ and say, "This game is making you feel frustrated, isn't it?"
and instead of screaming and kicking off, he'll agree and go on to
explain why it's frustrating him."

Setting and Enforcing Boundaries

Empathy and validation can go hand in hand with setting and enforcing boundaries. They are important for the well-being of all children, especially so for children with ODD, ADHD, and OCD. Boundaries provide structure and expectations; they should be both clear and reasonable, which alleviates uncertainty and any anxiety related to that. With appropriate and clearly enforced boundaries in place, children will know exactly what is acceptable and what is not, and it helps with their emotional development.

How to Set and Communicate Boundaries

Let's take a look at some practical tips to help you set and communicate boundaries (Ehmke, 2017; Growing Early Minds, 2019):

- Involve your child in the rule-setting process and have an open discussion about what behavior is acceptable and what isn't. This is also a great opportunity to agree on consequences.
- The rules, limits, and responsibilities should be clear and easy to understand. Make sure they are aligned with your family's values so children understand behavioral expectations.
- Use direct, specific language rather than vague directives that invite confusion over what constitutes acceptable conduct.
- Consistency is really important here. Once a boundary is set, make sure you enforce it every time, not just when it suits you or when you can be bothered to follow through. Everyone has hard days; they will only get harder if you let things slide and offer mixed messages.
- Convey rules with firm yet calm and compassionate authority that models regulated behavior and minimizes reactive escalation.

- Provide frequent encouragement and acknowledgment when children demonstrate responsibility or self-restraint, to positively reinforce those efforts.
- Resist pressure from entitlement attitudes by holding age- and developmentally-appropriate expectations around skill levels while scaffolding increasing independence.
- Prepare children for the real world by gradually expanding their freedom and imposing natural consequences that are logically tied to their behaviors.
- Check that your own boundaries surrounding affection or privacy are mirrored back by your children as they learn to set their own limits.

Teaching Self-Regulation Skills

Self-regulation for children and adults is the "ability to regulate their emotions, thoughts, and behavior to enable them to act in positive ways toward a goal" (Birth to 5 Matters, 2021). It's important to note that this is not a skill that we are born with—it is something we must develop and nurture into adulthood. Kids from the ages of 0–11 cannot self-regulate because their brains are not developed enough to do so. It is the parent's job, then, to model regulation to the child. Modeling should occur during the parents' own big feelings and when the child is having an episode. This is called *co-regulation,* and it is the foundation for teaching children self-regulating skills.

Co-regulation is the biggest thing that parents miss—especially when they are frustrated. When the parent escalates with the child, then no one is able to listen because everyone is heightened emotionally. As a parent, if you feel that level of frustration in which you have risen to your child's level of emotion, then it is absolutely okay to walk away and take a break as long as the situation is safe to do so. Once you have taken a moment to calm down, come back to the situation at hand and deal with it then in a better frame of mind.

It is okay to make mistakes and apologize to the child for making the mistake. This not only strengthens the bond between you but also models healthy problem-solving behaviors that your child will adopt. It is human to have big feelings and make mistakes; it is healthy for all involved to apologize after.

Let's take a look at the developmental stages again and explore the different age-appropriate techniques that can be implemented to help with the development of self-regulation:

Age/stage	Self- and co-regulation techniques
Toddlers (1–3)	• Play emotional matching and labeling games. • Provide sensory outlets like playdoh or soft toys. • Use timings and warnings for transitions. • Model taking deep breaths when frustrated.
Preschoolers (3–5)	• Read stories modeling self-soothing. • Teach breathing exercises with bubbles or pinwheels. • Provide positive reinforcement. • Use visual charts tracking emotional progress.
School age (6–12)	• Worksheets identifying escalation levels and triggers. • Learn techniques for questioning negative assumptions. • Create a personalized sensory space for time-outs. • Practice progressive muscle relaxation for panic prevention.
Teens (13–18)	• Establish emotional check-in routines. • Look into ideal mental health apps for mood tracking/coping. • Work together on anger management plans and go-to supports. • Weigh the pros and cons of therapies and medications if mood disorders appear.

Building Resilience and Coping Skills

Finally, let's consider the importance of building resilience and coping skills not just in our children but in ourselves as well. As we have uncovered, explosive behavior in children stems from a lack of these kinds of skills, and these aren't the kinds of skills you can teach without having worked on them yourself, too. If you cannot cope with stress in a healthy way, how do you expect to be able to teach your child? It's time to work together with your child to nurture resilience between you both.

Take a look at the following strategies to help you develop your resilience (American Psychological Association, 2020; Mind, 2022):

- **Supportive relationships:** Surround yourself with caring individuals who can offer guidance during difficult times. Sometimes, just having someone listen can relieve stress and help you cope, and you can offer that to your child, too.
- **Set goals:** You can find purpose and meaning in each day through achievable goals, uplifting activities, and a sense of accomplishment. You can help yourself and your child to find an activity that gives that sense of purpose and accomplishment.
- **Reflecting on the past:** Reflect on how you overcame obstacles in the past, think about the effective skills and behaviors that built resilience in that scenario, and how you can use them again. Do this with your child when they are facing an obstacle.
- **Positive mindset:** Remain hopeful about the future even when you cannot change painful aspects of the present or past. Looking ahead will help you to become more adaptable. Help your child to plan and envision the future positively instead of staying entrenched in negativity.

- **Take care of yourself:** Take care of your physical and mental health through self-care practices like healthy eating, adequate sleep, exercise, stress management techniques, and making time for hobbies. Model this for your child and help them to do the same.
- **Be proactive:** Take action in the face of adversity by facing problems head-on to improve situations within your control rather than ignoring issues. Encourage your child to be proactive, too, and get ahead of problems.
- **Access social support and professional services:** If you feel unable to progress alone, consider therapy or counseling to build your resilience muscle. There is no shame in seeking external guidance for you or your child— we all need help sometimes.

Strong coping skills will provide both you and your child with the internal and external support that you need to be resilient over time. When you have a strong sense of resilience, you will be more adaptable in the face of adversity, hard times, and big feelings. You will have better mechanisms for avoiding overwhelm and anxiety and better emotional regulation skills.

POSITIVE PARENTING TECHNIQUES

To close this chapter, let's take a look at positive parenting techniques that you can adopt that will help you improve the future behavior of your child.

Emphasizing Positive Reinforcement

Positive reinforcement is the reinforcement of stimuli to increase future behavior (O'Neal. et al., 2019). This involves offering praise, rewards, and incentives in place of punishment. Let's take a look at a list of examples of positive reinforcement in action:

- When a child finishes all of their dinner, they get ice cream.
- When a parent gives a baby attention, the baby smiles at them.
- When a child keeps their hands and feet to themselves, they get praise or a treat.
- When a child gets dressed for school independently without nagging reminders, they can pick a fun breakfast like pancakes or waffles.
- When a child assists in yard cleanup without complaints, the family enjoys an evening picnic outside with the child's favorite foods afterward.

The goal of positive reinforcement is to focus on highlighting and praising the behaviors that the parent wants to see more of rather than simply criticizing the negative behaviors. Children love to be recognized, praised, and given treats. The incentive will help them to intentionally choose positive behavior because they look forward to the praise.

Here are some examples of positive reinforcement techniques parents can implement to encourage constructive behavior:

- Praise good sharing, empathy, or patience. Make sure you label the positive behavior so the child knows exactly what triggered your response, and add smiles, high fives, and enthusiasm.
- You could use encouragement charts or sticker systems that eventually grant rewards like special outings or game time based on their progress.
- Display their artwork that they worked hard and concentrated on.
- Praise them for a willingness to compromise instead of taking control and being bossy or stubborn.

Fostering Emotional Intelligence

Emotional intelligence is "the ability to understand, use, and manage your own emotions in positive ways to relieve stress, communicate effectively, empathize with others, overcome challenges, and defuse conflict" (Segal, 2023). Clearly, these are all things our explosive children struggle with, as we have uncovered this far into the book.

Emotional intelligence is a skill that you can help your child develop, just like any other. Here are some ways parents can help build emotional intelligence in children:

Label emotions:

- Label your own feelings and interpretations of others' emotions, e.g., "I feel very frustrated when the kitchen is so messy," or "Hunter seems sad, his head is down, and he's crying quietly after someone took his toy."
- When you are reading a story, you can ask your child how characters are feeling and what clues indicate those emotions. What is the character saying? What is their body language?
- Use an expanded vocabulary to describe emotions like happy and sad, and watch your child's vocabulary and emotional understanding grow.

Mirror emotional displays:

- If your child is feeling disappointed, come down to their level and show them the disappointment mirrored in your own expression. Reflect your child's negative emotions back calmly and with empathy, allowing them to see feelings manifested externally, then discuss constructive responses.

Process intense emotions:

- After outbursts, gently explore what triggered big feelings once they have calmed down. Make sure you handle these conversations respectfully without blame or shame.

Role-play social situations:

- This is perfect if your child has dolls or toy characters. You can roleplay situations with the toys and practice reading social cues and appropriate responses. You can use the time after play to discuss why certain reactions matter.

The objective is increasing emotional awareness, intelligence around handling feelings constructively, and social sensitivity—all crucial for relationships and social development.

Encouraging Social Skills Development

Explosive behavior often reaches much further than the four walls of the family home. Children who struggle with these kinds of episodes tend to have fewer friends and difficulty navigating social situations due to their lack of social skills (Li, 2020).

When discussing emotional intelligence above, we touched on the idea of role-playing social situations during play. Doing this regularly will help to set your child up for social success because you can teach them real skills while having fun. Things like taking turns are also extremely important—don't let your child dominate the game, even if that feels easier. Teach them how to compromise.

You will also find that if your child is having any social problems, they might come out during the role-playing game as your child tries to process what is happening in the real world. This is a great opportunity to let them have a social "do-over." You can gently guide your child to learn social nuances and practice responses in a calm, low-pressure environment.

Teachers can also play a part in helping your child to build on their social skills. If they are struggling to make friends, teachers can pair them up with other children who may be suitable playmates.

Your parenting strategies and skills matter tremendously to your child and help to manage their explosive behavior. Over time and with consistent effort, you can transform your relationship with your child, have a better understanding of what influences their behavior, and take proactive steps to teach them skills like improving their emotional intelligence. In the next chapter, we will dive more deeply into communication and conflict resolution. The goal is to create a supportive family environment, maintain balance, and nurture *all* family members.

CHAPTER 4

COMMUNICATION AND CONFLICT RESOLUTION

"You hate me!" Rowan screeched.

Meredith sighed and took a step toward the boy, whose anger was like a dark cloud about his shoulders, "I don't hate you, Rowan," she pleaded.

"Yes, you do! You're always yelling and bossing me around! You hate me, and you're horrible!"

This was becoming an increasingly common episode in their home. Meredith would tell Rowan it was time to get off his Playstation, and Rowan would become so enraged with her.

"It's the same bedtime every day!" Meredith would yell. "If you just keep an eye on the time, you'd notice when it was time to come off. I wouldn't have to remind you, and this fight wouldn't have to happen every *single* day! It's exhausting!"

Meredith believed that her son should be better with his time management. Rowan would get so engrossed in his game that when Meredith interrupted him and told him he had to immediately stop, turn it off, and get ready for bed, he would fly into a dark rage almost instantly. Meredith wanted to confiscate the PlayStation. Rowan wanted his mom to stop bossing him around. Neither of them were communicating effectively.

Communication is absolutely vital in any relationship, especially the relationship between parent and child. As we have learned so far, children are not born with these social skills; we teach them, and we model them.

One evening, after a particularly nasty shouting match, Meredith dragged herself back upstairs and knocked tentatively on Rowan's door.

"Can we talk?" she asked him quietly. "Can we come up with a plan to make this better?"

This moment was the gateway to a more healthy form of communication between the two. Meredith learned that her son needed help with his time management and that he needed a warning every five or ten minutes leading up to the time he was expected to come off his PlayStation. They agreed to set a new routine that they both worked hard at. The explosive episodes seemed to stop almost instantly now that Rowan was getting some help easing into the transition. Meredith would often sit on the edge of Rowan's bed for the last ten minutes of his timer and watch him play, which became their special time together in the evenings.

Communication can have a profound impact on an explosive child's behavior and family dynamics. In this chapter, we're going to learn effective communication strategies, how to use active listening and empathy, and introduce you to the power of collaborative problem-solving. You can be like Meredith and Rowan; you can overcome communication challenges and build a better relationship with your child.

EFFECTIVE COMMUNICATION STRATEGIES

Let's begin by looking at effective communication strategies. In order to improve communication, you must first identify what is preventing you from communicating effectively in the first place, construct a safe communication environment, and adapt your communication styles.

Identifying Communication Barriers

Take another look at the exchange between Rowan and Meredith at the start of the chapter. They were each having a very different conversation: Rowan felt personally attacked by his mother; the urgency and frustration in her voice made him believe she was always cross with him. Meredith was baffled by how Rowan associated being asked to turn off his PlayStation with her hating him; she simply wanted him to take some personal ownership of his time-keeping.

Miscommunication, misunderstandings, and assumptions are littered throughout communication in families with explosive children. Everyone is having a different conversation, just like Meredith and Rowan. Explosive children may mistakenly believe that their parents don't care about their stress or triggers because they don't understand them, and parents might misperceive explosions as deliberate or manipulative and focus on disrespect and disobedience rather than the unmet needs or underdeveloped skills. This can result in daily friction and misunderstanding between parent and child, disrupting their bond.

A classic example of miscommunication between parent and child is when a parent tells their child to "Please behave yourself today." This directive is much too vague for the child and doesn't give them any information on what they should be doing. The parent will inevitably feel frustrated later when the child misbehaves: "I thought I told you to behave yourself today!"

Let's take a look at some practical exercises to help you identify and address your specific communication barriers:

Active Listening

This can be a fun activity to do with your kid. Decide which of you will be the speaker and which will be the listener. Set a two-minute timer. During this time, the speaker will talk on a chosen topic, and the listener will listen.

The listener is tasked with concentrating on understanding. They have to use eye contact, nodding, and facial expressions without interrupting. After the timer stops, the listener gets the chance to summarize and comment. They should think of open-ended questions they can ask the speaker.

Then, switch roles and play from the other perspective.

If listening is something that you struggle with, you might find yourself feeling impatient with this exercise. This shows that you need to work on your active listening skills with your child, which will help you have more effective communication.

Model Behavior

Think about a recent incident when your child lost their temper —perhaps they refused to pick up their toys or do their homework. Close your eyes and play the incident through, paying attention to your own facial expressions, body language, and tone of voice. Were you snapping and short with your child? Were your eyebrows drawn in annoyance? What kind of language did you use—were you calm and helpful or demanding and controlling?

Now, I want you to picture the same incident in your mind, but this time, change your body language, facial expression, and tone of voice. How might that have changed the outcome of the episode?

We will return to this idea again and again throughout this book. Modeling behavior is one of the most effective ways you can change the dynamic with your children. If you are always tense and dismissive of your child because you are busy, distracted, or frustrated with them, then they will reflect that behavior right back at you. If you yell all the time and expect your child to remain calm, that will not happen.

Communication Quiz

Taking a communication quiz is a great way to figure out where your strengths and weaknesses lie. Use the results to work on different areas of your communication. There are lots available online, or you could try this one:

https://reallifefamilies.org/wp-content/uploads/2016/12/assertive-communication-quiz.pdf

1, 2, 3 Magic

1, 2, 3 Magic is a really simple exercise. You give your child three chances to stick to a rule, and if they are still breaking the rule by the third chance, you end the activity for now.

Let's say your child is going to go ride their bike, and the rule is they need their helmet, but they don't want to wear it. The parent brings the child over and says, "Nicki, the rule is that you are supposed to wear a helmet while riding your bike. You will have three chances to put on your helmet, or we will be done riding for the day, and you can do it on a different day. This is your first warning."

Nicki puts on the helmet, and the parent walks back inside. Nicki then takes the helmet off, and the parent looks back outside and sees that Nicki does not have the helmet on. The parent says, "Nicki, this is number two. The rule is you have to have your helmet on while riding your bike. You have one last chance. If it is not on the entire time you are riding your bike, we will stop riding the bike and will have to do something else, and you can get the bike back tomorrow."

Then, you give the child a different activity to do. This is not an exercise that will work 100% of the time. There are kids that it will and will not work for.

Make a Chart

This is a simple chart that lets both you and your child know what they can do as an alternative when they start to feel a certain way. There are examples in the chart below, but you should create your own, tailored to your child's personality and behaviors.

In the first column, list the behavior the child is showing, and in the second column, make a list of all the activities they can do instead.

Behaviors the child is showing	Activities they could do instead
Boredom	• Puzzles • Reading • Playing outside • Playing a board game
Picking on siblings	• Ask parents what they can do instead • Going outside to relieve frustration
Frustration	• Using legos or blocks to build and being able to knock them down • Getting something to eat • Going outside and running around • Screaming into a pillow • Venting to a parent or a friend

Slow Down, Take a Breath

When you start to feel steam coming out of your ears or off the top of your head, this is the time to take a step back, breathe, and analyze the situation. You can even walk away from the situation to help yourself calm down. Once you take a couple of deep breaths, you can come back to the situation and look at the "problem" from your child's point of view, which both the parent and child can problem-solve. If the child is too young, the parent can give the child choices to help them with the problem-solving.

For example, your child is yelling right when they get in the door from school. Using this technique, you will slow down and not yell at the child. Instead, you will stop and observe and think back to what school was like for you. At school, your child has to keep their emotions in check and not throw tantrums or yell. When they express big feelings either in the car or at home, they are in a safe environment to "let loose" and get all these uncomfortable emotions out of their system.

Constructing a Safe Communication Environment

The environment sets the tone for communication—always. When anyone feels that they are in a space of judgment, they will close themselves off to protect themselves. This is especially true for our explosive children, who struggle with negative feelings and their self-esteem.

If you want your child to open up to you, it is important to create a safe, non-judgmental space for them where they don't have to worry about criticism, embarrassment, or disappointment. Be compassionate and use empathy and active listening skills; your child will feel safe to be vulnerable, and you will open up your understanding instead of sticking to your rigid beliefs about their behavior.

Tips for Establishing and Maintaining a Safe Communication Environment

The following is not an exhaustive list, but there are some tips below that should help you in creating and maintaining an environment that makes your child feel safe, valued, and listened to (Axtell, 2019; Woudstra, 2022):

- **Make emotional check-ins a priority:** This could be something as simple as always discussing thoughts and feelings over dinner or scheduling a specific emotional check-in time during the week.
- **Show your child that they can rely on you:** If they ask you to keep something they've said confidential, then do (unless, of course, there is a safety risk). If you promise not to get mad or tell them off for admitting they broke something, then don't. Teach them that problem-solving and compassion are the aim of these conversations, not punishment and control.
- **Explore the concept of active listening with your child:** This is a skill that both of you will benefit and we will delve more deeply into it later in the chapter. Take it in turn to really listen to each other without interruption when communicating.
- **Ask thoughtful questions:** Questions can often hold a huge amount of criticism: "Why would you get the glitter out when you know I have just vacuumed?" sounds much more accusatory than: "What were you trying to make with your craft supplies?"
- **Keep an eye out for nonverbal cues:** Kids show their discomfort during conversations just as adults do, so keep watch for their body language telling you they need a break and respect that. They might not be ready to talk about the issue right now; let them know that you are ready to listen

when they are ready to talk. This will help them to feel secure and that you have their best interests at heart.

- **Offer them validation:** We've touched on this already; validation is huge, especially when behaviors feel like they are out of our control. Tell your child: "I know that it was really hard for you to tell me that you spilled the glitter all over the carpet; thank you for being honest."
- **Discuss and problem-solve together:** Including your child in coming up with a solution to the problem helps them to feel that their voice is valued. "How can we work together to clean up the craft supplies?"

Case Study

Elliot used to have awful meltdowns after school. Sometimes, it started on the walk home, but more often, it began 10 minutes or so after getting home. There would be a minor trigger—his iPad wasn't charged, the dog wouldn't sit with him, or the sky was blue. His parents were feeling strained and unsure of how to proceed. They couldn't understand why he was so calm at school but so angry at home.

After getting some advice, they implemented emotional check-ins over dinner. Over time, Elliot started talking more and more about his school day. He mentioned his lessons, his friends, and playing at break time. One day, his mom asked him about lunch break, and he told her he only ever ate one bite of food and then had to leave the cafeteria to get away from the overwhelming bustle of people.

His parents realized that Elliot's after-school moods were probably due to his lack of eating all day and spoke with the school. They were able to find somewhere for Elliot to eat with only one or two friends instead of the cafeteria, and the after-school outburst quickly stopped. Having a safe environment to communicate in helped Elliot and his parents get to the bottom of his behavior.

Adapting Communication Styles

Every child will respond differently to different communication styles. It is your job as their parent or caregiver to adapt your communication style to match what the child needs in the moment.

In this scenario, consider your communication skills as a set of tools. In a toolbox, you generally have the same variations of tools. Sometimes, you use your hammer to put nails in things, and other times, you use your hammer to take the nails out. Communication styles are like the hammer; sometimes, you need to adapt how you use them.

There are many different ways you can communicate the same point. Here, we are going to explore the following:

- **Direct:** This involves using clear, concise language and emphasizing key details.
- **Supportive:** In this case, you would use a warm, compassionate tone and focus on the emotional needs of the communication.
- **Instructive:** As more of an educational approach, this form helps to problem-solve.

Direct communication styles are best used for explaining family rules and values and giving clear instructions for specific behavioral expectations. When you are responding to your child's worries, you should use supportive communication. This is best used when validating your child's feelings during conflicts or meltdowns. Instructive communication tends to come after the meltdown; here, you teach your child how to identify their triggers and teach them coping strategies.

This is an example of how you would use each style in the same scenario:

- **Direct:** "Hitting and mean words are never okay. Use gentle hands and be kind with your actions and speaking."
- **Supportive:** "I know you feel really angry right now. I'm here to listen and help."
- **Instructive:** "When you feel this overwhelmed, deep breaths can help your body and mind calm down. Shall we practice together?"

Context is vital when deciding which communication style you need to lead within an interaction. Adapting between these styles will help you to handle explosive behavior in a more systematic way while also giving your child a structure that they can rely on.

ACTIVE LISTENING AND EMPATHY

A key aspect of communication that we have already touched upon is active listening. This is a form of communication that goes beyond simply listening; it involves appropriate eye contact, watching for nonverbal cues, asking open-ended questions, and paraphrasing and reflecting back what has been said, among other things (Cuncic, 2022). Implementing tactics of active listening and empathy can help you strengthen your relationship with your child while supporting them through their explosive behavior.

Fundamentals of Active Listening

The goal of active listening is to fully engage with the speaker and hear what they are saying. It is an active process that involves much more than simply sitting quietly and listening. Let's take a look at what you can do to improve your active listening (Cuncic, 2022; Mind Tools Content Team, 2022):

Give Them Your Full Attention

When your child speaks, you need to first concentrate completely on the conversation ahead of you. Put down any distractions, like your phone, and keep your attention trained on your child.

Use Affirming Body Language

Use your body language to let your child know that you are listening; think of making eye contact, nodding, and leaning closer toward them. Come down to their eye level so that they can be sure they have your full attention.

Verbal Signs of Listening

This means more than simply agreeing or making affirming grunts. The trick here is to paraphrase and repeat back the point that your child is making, which makes them feel validated and heard. If you are talking about their explosive behavior, ask them, "What happens in your body when you start to feel angry?"

Ask Questions

Open-ended questions are important here. Lean into what your child is telling you and ask simple, curious questions that keep them talking and opening up. Asking the right kinds of questions can often lead you to new information.

When you implement these main components of active listening, you can completely shift the dynamic of a conversation with your child. We are often so busy thinking and planning ahead, worrying about work, finances, or what's for dinner that we don't actually hear them when our children chat to us. To us, they might be talking about something nonsensical, but when a child tries to convey something that is important to them, and we brush it off, it only widens that communication gap between us and makes the difficult conversations that much harder. Listening to your child day-to-day will foster a sense of trust between you both; they will learn that they can rely on you and open up to you when it matters the most.

Cultivating Empathy

Empathy is defined in the Merriam-Webster dictionary as "the action of understanding, being aware of, being sensitive to, and vicariously experiencing the feelings, thoughts, and experience of another" (n.d.). Based on everything we have discussed thus far about understanding your child and their behavior, clearly, empathy has a huge role to play here. As parents and caregivers, it is absolutely crucial that we look beyond the surface judgment of our children's explosive outbursts and look at their inner workings and motivations in order to help them.

If empathy is something you struggle with, there are ways you can develop a deeper empathy. Let's consider the concept of role-playing once again, although this time, through perspective-taking. If you can, get your child to play with you and take on each others' role during a meltdown to see if you can tap into one another's feelings and struggles in the moment. You could also consider taking up journalling to help you to access feelings of empathy. Consider the following journaling prompts:

- Think about a time when you felt embarrassed or ashamed as a child when your deepest feelings were criticized or dismissed. What can you do differently to validate your child's emotional experiences to prevent them from feeling the way that you did?
- Make a list of the behaviors in your child that frustrate you most right now. Then, think about what might be driving these disruptive patterns. How can this reframe and change your response to your child next time they show the behavior?

- Were there any family traditions or rituals that made you feel deeply loved, valued, or understood growing up? Using this a guide, how can you nurture your child through consistent empathy?

Bridging Emotional Gaps

As we know, explosive behavior stems from a lack of emotional regulation, skills, and understanding. These huge emotional gaps can be bridged! Children, at their core, are looking for acknowledgment and acceptance for who they are. They need to know that what they feel matters and that you aren't simply looking for a picture-perfect child who knows how to behave "appropriately" like a perfect china doll.

This is why validating their feelings is so crucial. They may be having these huge verbal and physical outbursts, which are not warranted, but the feelings behind those outbursts are absolutely normal and acceptable. It's up to us to help them close the emotional gap.

So, how do we do that?

Strategies for Communicating Understanding and Support

Using some of the following strategies, you can learn to communicate understanding and support to your child (Greene, 2018; Jack, 2023; Lopes, 2023):

- **"I hear" statements:** It's important to express what emotions or issues you are seeing based on the child's words or behaviors. For example, you might say, "I hear this playground problem really embarrassed or upset you..."
- **"I feel" statements:** Using these statements helps you to share your genuine emotional reactions to the situation

empathetically. You might say, "I feel sad realizing how hurt and scared this is making you..."

- **"I understand" statements:** Understanding validates the difficulty behind what your child faces at their developmental level. Say things like, "I understand needing some space when everything feels too overwhelming..."
- **Ask, "How can I help?":** After reflecting back on the child's experience, you should offer tangible solution-focused support. A simple "How can I help you work through this to feel better?" will go a long way.
- **"We've got this" assurances:** Finally, reassure your child that you are in their corner. They should believe that you are both in this together with unconditional love and support, regardless of their behavior. Use phrases like, "We've got this—I'm here whenever you need me."

THE POWER OF COLLABORATIVE PROBLEM-SOLVING

Let's turn our attention to collaborative problem-solving now. Notice the word "collaborative." Your child's problems are not theirs alone, nor are they a problem for you alone to fix. You are a team in this as you are in all things while they are young, and together, you can work through explosive behavior and other problems that arise.

Introducing Collaborative Problem-Solving

According to Green (n.d.), collaborative problem-solving is figuring out where the child is having a hard time following through with the instructions, coming together (both parent and child) to problem-solve, and helping the child to excel with that specific instruction, and not to modify the behavior. Again, this is about discarding the idea that the child is simply being non-compliant and understanding that there is a very real reason behind the behavior—a problem that needs to be solved.

There are three steps in this approach to problem-solving:

- **Empathizing with the child:** You've worked on this skill already! Make sure that you express an understanding of how difficult the trigger and outburst are for the child. Use your active listening skills and validate how they are feeling.
- **Defining the problem:** Your child might need your help here in figuring out what the exact trigger was. Discuss everything that happened leading up to the explosion, and don't forget to look beneath the reason your child gives: If they lost their temper because George went to play with Ellie instead of them, the problem isn't George or Ellie; it's that your child felt left out and needs connection and friendship.
- **Brainstorming solutions together:** This is the most important part—coming up with a solution *together*. When you give them the answer to their problem, the outburst will happen again and again. Engaging their brain and discussing the solution with them will help them to remember the solution in the future, hopefully *before* the outburst takes place.

Now that we've covered the idea of collaborative problem-solving let's look more closely at your role in this and the most effective ways that you can help your child while they are fostering their independence and collaboration skills.

Role of Parents in Facilitating Solutions

You matter tremendously to the emotional growth of your child. Everything that you do or say has an impact on your child's development. That might feel like a lot of pressure, but it's actually a blessing. So, how can you use this incredible blessing to help your child in finding solutions?

There is a fine line here that you need to tread carefully. You get the final word because you are the ultimate authority here; therefore, you hold the accountability. Your challenge is to scaffold your child's critical thinking and give them some decision-making power while still maintaining the boundaries around safety and values. This is about finding the balance between leadership and collaboration.

Effective strategies here include:

- Taking the lead and guiding the discussion rather than allowing them to go off on rambling tangents.
- Reminding them of the bigger picture when they get distracted.
- Keeping the discussion focused, productive, and solution-oriented.
- Using your active listening and ask open-ended, insightful questions that prompt them to think deeper.

The parent's role here is to guide the problem-solving process without dominating it. You have to allow them the freedom to explore their own critical thinking and direct them toward finding a productive solution.

Building Long-Term Conflict Resolution Skills

As you are working on these core problem-solving skills, it's important to keep in mind that this is not about finding immediate relief from conflict with your child. Collaborative problem-solving skills are going to serve them well for the rest of their adult lives; they will be able to employ conflict-resolution skills in the workplace and socially, thanks to the time you devote to them now, giving them much more opportunity for success and fulfillment.

Yes, you will help them handle their meltdowns and triggers more effectively right now. But in a broader sense, you will be teaching them how to verbalize their needs and discomforts constructively with their friends and future colleagues. Instead of having huge emotional explosions, they will learn adaptability when problems arise. Self-control and self-esteem will both rise along with their social skills and confidence. They will learn how to be resilient in the face of tough problems and will find a way to navigate through instead of giving up and blowing up.

Daily, explosive episodes centered around conflict and inflexibility seemed to rule Jayden's life. Every one of his parents, caregivers, teachers, and specialists were concerned that he was going to end up facing serious social and academic repercussions as he grew older. He played alone more and more during the school day, and most interactions with his peers ended up in an episode of rage and arguing.

Jayden's parents decided to focus on his problem-solving and conflict-resolution skills in an attempt to help him avoid the loneliness that lay in his path ahead. Jayden's parents utilized the active listening, empathy, and communication/parenting styles in this book. His parents were able to scaffold Jayden and begin to teach him new strategies for problem-solving that didn't end in him being stubborn, inflexible, and screaming. Jayden was paired with other children at school under the watchful eye of his one-to-one support worker. Hiccups occurred, as they always do in life, but Jayden was able to use his newfound communication skills to take part in games and play with his peers—something that was unheard of until now. There was also a marked improvement in his school work as he transferred those problem-solving skills to the classroom and found the confidence to try the math problems, even if he didn't always understand them.

You see, these skills aren't just for beating meltdowns at home, and explosions aren't the only behavior we can improve with these techniques. We can be better parents, and our children can be happier, more well-rounded individuals if we just put in the work outlined in this book.

At the start of the chapter, when Meredith took herself back upstairs to talk with Rowan, she opened up the door to effective communication, problem-solving, and conflict resolution. She realized that the unhealthy rhythm of their current dynamic was not going to change until she took the initiative as the parent. However, there was much more work to be done after they improved their communication. Next, they needed to work on managing Rowan's behavior. In the next chapter, you will find much-needed insights into behavioral management and disciplined approaches tailored to the needs of explosive children.

DEAR VALUED READER

Did you know that when you talk to kids about their feelings, they grow up understanding emotions better? That's something Daniel J. Siegel, a famous author, once said. In "Raising an Explosive Child Like a Pro," we talk a lot about understanding and handling big emotions, especially in kids with challenges like ADHD, OCD, or ODD.

But here's a little secret: helping others can actually make you happier and healthier. So, I've got a small favor to ask of you. It won't cost you a penny, and it'll take less than a minute, but it could change someone's life.

Imagine a parent struggling with their child's explosive behaviors. They might feel lost, just like you might have felt before. They need help, and your review of this book could be the guiding light they're searching for.

Here's how you can make a huge difference:

Leave a Review: Just scan the QR code below and share your thoughts about the book. Your honest review could be the help another parent or caregiver desperately needs.

By leaving a review, you're not just sharing your opinion; you're giving hope and help to someone out there who feels overwhelmed. You're part of a greater community of parents, grandparents, and caregivers that supports each other, and that's something really special.

I'm here to support your journey toward a stress-free home with tactics, lessons, and strategies you will love. Thank you for being a part of this mission, for being awesome, and for making a difference.

   - Your biggest fan, Gigi GrayHaven

P.S. - Remember, sharing is caring! If you think this book can help another parent or caregiver, spread the love and pass it along. You never know whose life you might change with a simple act of kindness.

Back to Our Regularly Scheduled Programming

Now, let's dive back into understanding and managing explosive behaviors in kids. Together, we're on this journey to create happier, healthier homes and hearts. Let's keep learning and growing!

Stay Awesome!

CHAPTER 5

BEHAVIORAL MANAGEMENT AND DISCIPLINE

I n a study that involved 62 years of collected data, psychologist Elizabeth Thompson Gershoff, Ph.D., found strong associa-tions between corporal punishment and negative behaviors such as increased child aggression and antisocial behavior (Gershoff, 2002). Corporal punishment has long been used as the go-to discipline method for children who misbehave. It has only been in recent generations that we have begun to shift away from this model, but, unfortunately, it is still often used today, along with many other traditional methods like time-outs and punishments.

As previously mentioned, these methods of discipline don't teach the child what they *should* be doing; they only tell the child what they have to stop doing, which leaves a void in their understanding and emotional development.

In this chapter, you're going to learn alternative, effective strategies to help you discipline your child and manage their tough behavior.

UNDERSTANDING AND IMPLEMENTING CONSEQUENCES

Typically, in parenting, consequences are seen as punishments for bad behavior. The idea is that the child is made to feel uncomfortable enough that they don't want to feel that way again and thus don't repeat the behavior that put them in that discomfort.

However, when looking at the principles of applied behavior analysis, we begin to understand that consequences can mean something more than this.

Rethinking Consequences

In reality, consequences are neither good or bad, but simply stimuli that reinforce future behavior (Cooper et al., 2020). In other words, all consequences intrinsically provoke more or less reoccurrence of associated behaviors—regardless of your moral lens. Explosive children are not going to make the connection between having an outburst and then being grounded or having their TV time taken away—punishing this behavior is only setting them up for failure because you aren't filling the gap where the negative behavior currently lives.

As we have learned, explosive behavior already reflects a level of distress within the child. If we automatically move to punish them for their behavior, we are risking damaging the parent-child relationship through resentment. This kind of parenting misses the mark because it does not teach the child what they should replace the negative behavior with. However, when we teach our children through positive reinforcement and rewarding behavior, this intrinsically motivates them to repeat that rewarding behavior. Using stimulus-behavior analysis rather than reflexive penalties rethinks consequences and produces real child development breakthroughs, which is the ultimate goal.

Let's take a look at some examples of typical vs. effective consequences for explosive children:

Typical parental responses	Effective parental responses
• Yelling harsh criticisms when an emotional meltdown occurs. • Spanking or physical discipline reactively mid-tantrum. • Grounding children to their room for angry outbursts. • Sticker charts only track problem behaviors in red.	• Remain calm using empathetic statements when upset arises. • Redirect tantrums into outlets like clenching Play-Doh or pillow screams. • Provide caring physical touch, words, or time/space preferred for co-regulation. • Reward responsibility like self-soothing deep breaths once composure is regained. • Praise positive opposites the moment fighting stops or kindness is shown.

Notice how the typical parenting responses only focus on the negative behavior, but the effective responses model calm, redirecting, and praise, which all encourage the child to learn a new way to behave.

Consistency in Applying Consequences

Remember, consequences are neither good or bad. That doesn't mean that consequences do not exist. If I pick up my mug carelessly and spill my tea on my laptop, the consequence is that my laptop is now broken. It sucks, and it might feel negative; the lesson here was that I need to stop having drinks around my laptop. Another example might be when I need to leave work early one day to go and watch my daughter's school play. If I work hard and get all my work finished early, the consequence is that I get to leave early—this one feels more positive, and the lesson I learned was to work hard to get rewarded at work with extra time off. The reality is that neither of these consequences was negative or positive; instead, they were natural outcomes of my own actions, and they both reinforced my behavior—being careful with drinks and working harder and more efficiently if I want time to go see my daughter at school.

When we are talking about consequences for our explosive children, it's important to emphasize consistency. According to the book *Applied Behavior Analysis*, "Behavior is the most sensitive to stimulates change that occurs immediately, after, or within a few seconds of response" (Conner, 2020, Pg 36). This means that the consistency of the consequence is the key to molding the child's behavior. If we react the same way every single time to a behavior, we are going to see more of a change in that behavior than if we were to be inconsistent with it.

For example, Tommy screams and stands in front of the TV when his brother Mark sits down to watch Tommy's favorite show with him. "It's my show! You can't watch it!" he yells, stamping his feet.

The first time this happens, Tommy's mom turns off the TV and tells Tommy that she understands that he is frustrated but that he can't control who gets to sit in the family room and watch what's on the TV. He doesn't get to watch his show if he's going to act that way. The second time this happens, Tommy's mom rolls her eyes, takes Mark out of the family room, and hands him the iPad to watch instead. This happens off and on again, and his mom doesn't understand why Tommy continues to scream at Mark every time he goes in to watch TV in the family room.

Tommy's mom was inconsistent with her discipline here. By allowing Tommy to kick Mark out of the family room, she was reinforcing the negative behavior. Tommy won't stop taking control of the TV in the family room; he doesn't connect his behavior with the outcomes because the outcome is different every time.

It's really important to always tell the child what you want them to do. If you have to say, "No, don't do that," remember to add what they can do instead. Tell the child what you would like to see them do so that they have something tangible to act on. For example, you can replace the statement "No, don't hit" with "Use gentle hands."

There will be times that you feel like it's easier not to maintain consistency; you might be really tired or sick, and you don't have the patience to remain calm or redirect tantrums. In those moments, it's important to remember that you are in this for the long haul. Future- you is going to be in for more hard times if you don't stay consistent even during challenging situations.

Here are some tips for when those moments happen:

- Learn some deep breathing strategies that you can use to help regulate yourself before you try to help regulate your child.
- Practice and prepare a "script" of what you might say to your child in different situations so you don't have to think on your feet when feeling overwhelmed.
- Set up a code word with your partner so you can swap places with them when you are feeling like you need a break.
- Seek support from other parents or parenting groups— knowing that you are not alone and other parents are having the same hard times can help you when you feel alone.

Tommy's mom eventually realized that she had to be consistent in order to help both her children enjoy the TV in the family room. She prepared her script in advance so she wouldn't get over- whelmed and give in. Then, every time Tommy had a meltdown, she would sit with him and calmly explain that the family room was for everyone and that he could not control if Mark wanted to come in to watch with him. She also left the iPad on the coffee table and told Tommy that if he wanted to watch his show on his own, he could take the iPad up to his room, where he was more than entitled to his own privacy. It took a few weeks, but one day, she poked her head into the family room and saw both boys comfy on the couch and watching TV together. When Tommy wanted to watch on his own, he would take himself upstairs and no longer rage at his brother.

Tailoring Consequences to Individual Needs

Every explosive child has their own personal triggers. As such, they will also need to have their own personalized consequences because one size does not fit all when it comes to OCD, ADHD, and ODD.

Using the skills that you learned earlier in the book, you can work out what your child's triggers are. Then, you can work on creating an intervention that is tailored to their needs in the moment. Consider using the ABC model (antecedent, behavior, consequence), and you will be able to match the appropriate consequence to the child's behavior.

For example, if your child has ADHD and struggles with impulse control, you can start to reward them for every moment you notice that they display patience—even if it's just for ten seconds. Rewarding patience instead of punishing impulsive behavior reinforces the behavior you want to see instead of making them even more frustrated and only increasing the problem behavior.

DISCIPLINE VS. PUNISHMENT

Punishment and discipline are two very different things, although they are often used interchangeably in parenting. According to the Merriam-Webster dictionary, *discipline* comes from *discipulus*, the Latin word for *pupil* (n.d.). The root of the word suggests that it originally meant "to teach." Somewhere along the way, it became confused with the word *punish*. However, we are going to unravel the two now.

Differentiating Discipline From Punishment

According to the Applied Behavior Analysis book, "Punishment is an action that will *decrease* future behavior" (Cooper, 2020). Punishment is negative and punitive, whereas discipline is positive and instructive.

Punishment tends to stem from the frustration of the parent and is based on their own upbringing rather than being used deliberately and intentionally to help the behavior. It is also just reinforcing to the person doling out the punishment; it doesn't do anything for the party receiving it. Discipline, on the other hand, is about scaffolding the child and helping them to build a better foundation. It is centered around problem-solving and communication. Consequences still exist in discipline but they are logically connected to the broken rules rather than being a random punishment.

For example, if your child can't sit still for dinner and causes disruption, the punishment might be that they are grounded for a week because that's your family's go-to punishment—however, you are punishing a child with too much energy by not allowing them to go outside and use that energy. There is no logical connection there. The solution here might be to let the child run around outside before dinner to release that energy before they have to sit and eat.

Let's take a closer look at the differences:

Punishment responses	Discipline responses
• Revoking all electronics indefinitely after one device-throwing episode: This fuels resentment without teaching self-regulation. • Harsh corporal punishment following aggressive hitting: Models physical retaliation and seems to condone violence. • Repeated timeouts: Alienates a sensitive child and exacerbates shame without building emotional intelligence.	• Granting outdoor play breaks when upset: Counters tension and practices constructive redirection. • Labeling: Saying things like, "I see frustration... let's breathe," validates the child's experience while demonstrating regulation. • Rewarding creativity or expressing intense emotions: Supplies healthy processing outlets.

It's important to focus compassionately on developing healthy coping habits in place of negative punishments, which fail to teach children long-term skills that help to reduce explosions.

Principles of Positive Discipline

According to Nelsen (2018), positive discipline "teaches important social and life skills in a manner that is deeply respectful and encouraging for both children and adults." You'll recognize most of these from what we have discussed so far, but let's take a look at the principles now (Nelsen, 2018):

- **Kindness and firmness:** Parents should balance compassion and empathy with upholding reasonable expectations and boundaries. The approach remains respectful yet strict, avoiding harshness.
- **Fostering connection and significance:** Positive relationships where children feel secure attachment and a sense of belonging translate to fewer behavioral issues. The aim of discipline is to preserve the parent–child emotional bond.

- **Teaches long-term life skills:** Rather than forcing superficial compliance, discipline focuses on instilling constructively managed emotions, communication, contribution, and problem-solving.
- **Uses natural consequences logically aligned to actions:** Rule violations directly cause related loss of privileges. This builds the child's internal motivation instead of using unrelated punishments that merely inflict pain.
- **Remains solution-focused instead of punishment-focused:** Supportive discipline concentrates on teaching, growth, and reconciliation—never shaming or blaming through criticism and penalties.

As you can see, having a connection is the focus of positive discipline. The goal is to nurture the child's sense of responsibility and capability by helping them to develop coping, social, and cooperation skills.

How can we put these principles into action? The examples below should give you a guide for using positive discipline in practice:

- **Kindness and firmness:** When your child is having a screaming tantrum, warmly redirect them to scream into a pillow instead.
- **Connection and significance:** When you are coming up with new rules or modifying the old ones as your child grows, speak with them about it and include them in the decision-making process here.
- **Teaches life skills:** During play, role-play apologizing and making amends after hurting someone's feelings to build empathy and conflict resolution abilities.

- **Logical consequences:** Have a child fix the toy they broke or earn money to replace it through extra chores. This reinforces accountability.
- **Solution-focused:** Brainstorm together how they can prevent waking the baby instead of just scolding loud indoor play. This teaches self-regulation skills.

Remember, the priority here is to avoid criticism. Instead, you are using these skills to help shape their behavior for the big wide world. This is much more constructive in the long run than using punishment. Punishment will only make the explosive behavior worse in the long run.

Avoiding Common Pitfalls

We all make mistakes, and we all fall back into old habits now and again—especially when we feel pushed to our limits. Having to patiently handle explosive behavior and nurture positive parenting skills when tired, stressed, and overwhelmed might sometimes feel impossible. If you can outline where you are most likely to slip up early, you can help yourself avoid these common pitfalls of positive parenting.

We touched on consistency already, but it really needs to be mentioned here again because it is one of the most common backward steps that a parent can take. Explosive children, in particular, rely on you for stability, so make sure that's your number one priority. Stick to your consequences and behavioral incentives; if you say you are going to do something, do it, and follow through with natural consequences soon after the unwanted behavior.

Often, parents get into power struggles with their little ones, and conflicts can escalate. This happens when we prioritize control over empathy. You are trying to teach your child that they cannot control other people and have their own way all the time, and then you also have to accept that you can't control them or have your own way all the time. But there is a balance here. Don't slip into enabling their behaviors simply because they are entitled to their own feelings. Redirect and educate them with all the tools you have gathered so far throughout this book. Don't get drawn into power struggles; prioritize nurturing over control.

Finally, remember to use discipline to your child's advantage. By that, I mean don't punish and remove privileges because they have an episode. Every meltdown is a teachable moment if you handle it correctly. Use the opportunity to teach them self-soothing techniques, discuss their triggers, and think of practical steps together to improve the skills that they are lacking.

Case Study

The Simmonds family noticed an increase in their son Aston's explosive behavior. At 10, they had hoped he would have learned some emotional regulation skills by now, and the relentless negative reports from school were getting everyone down. The school suggested family counseling.

After a few sessions, Aston's parents decided to give these techniques a try. They stopped yelling and punishing Aston for his outbursts and tried to offer him praise once he calmed down instead. The dynamic between the family shifted dramatically, and soon, Aston's outbursts were practically non-existent.

TAILORED BEHAVIORAL THERAPY TECHNIQUES

Sometimes, explosive behavior is beyond what we can manage alone at home as parents. Thankfully, there is tailored behavioral therapy support out there with trained professionals who want to help your child just as much as you do.

Introduction to Behavioral Therapy for Explosive Children

Behavioral therapy includes scientifically validated techniques that will directly address the explosive behavior and the motivations behind it. There are different kinds of behavioral therapy you can choose from; it is up to you to find which one will suit your child and family's needs best.

Functional Family Therapy

Specifically created for teenagers displaying behavioral issues, functional family therapy (FFT) offers families constructive skill-building aligned with explosive children's needs. This time-limited approach tends to cover around 12–14 sessions and integrates cognitive and interpersonal components. The aim is to tangibly improve behavior and family dynamics (Guarnotta & Troy, 2023).

First, FFT therapists focus intensively on strengthening empathy, communication, and trust within relationships through modeling and practice. They then move on to expanding emotional intelligence, self-control strategies, conflict resolution tactics, and problem-solving abilities in children alongside their parents. Finally, they help to prevent future crises by learning to anticipate potential pitfalls and introducing families to community resources as lifelong support.

Countless studies confirm FFT's effectiveness in transforming volatile adolescents by treating the family system, not just symptoms—studies such as that carried out by Thomas Sexton and Charles W Turner: "The effectiveness of functional family therapy for youth with behavioral problems in a community practice setting" (2010). Participants learn how to pragmatically resolve problems while feeling validated and heard at the same time.

Applied Behavior Analysis

Applied behavior analysis (ABA) offers families research-backed interventions tailored to individual challenges (Behavioral Innovations, n.d.). This customized approach first assesses a child's behaviors systematically to pinpoint which skills (or lack of) are interfering with their quality of life. Then, board certified specialists design targeted treatment plans that apply proven learning techniques toward goals that the families help to select for meaningfulness.

One-on-one sessions make use of parenting guidance to align home and therapy progress. There are also data-driven experiments that ensure effectiveness; adjustments are made until positive outcomes emerge. Verbal, academic, social, emotional, and self-care skills have all been shown to improve through consistent ABA scaffolding (Behavioral Innovations, n.d.).

For explosive children, ABA builds communication and regulation abilities. Parents also gain the tools they need to promote cooperation while preventing enabled entitlement. Though intensive, this validated framework cultivates child independence for long-term success, granting families some much-needed peace at home.

Cognitive Behavioral Therapy

Cognitive behavioral therapy (CBT) applies research-verified techniques addressing problematic thoughts, emotions, and behaviors through goal-directed, skills-building counseling. By first identifying lagging abilities contributing to outbursts like poor emotional regulation or communication gaps, CBT providers compassionately teach tailored antidotes (Andersen et al., 2016).

Parents receive guidance on how to respond constructively to their child's meltdowns through empathy, incentives, and consistency. Kids gain hands-on practice conquering anxiety triggers, managing disappointment calmly, resolving interpersonal conflicts, and more alongside supportive challenges. Tailored CBT assignments then generalize tools applied in session to everyday scenarios while tracking and celebrating incremental wins.

Multiple studies confirm CBT's effectiveness in improving mental health and resilience long-term by aligning intervention to specific needs, not symptoms alone (Hoffman et al., 2012). Though gradual, empowered self-efficacy blossoms through compassionate CBT guidance as families discover breakthroughs together that might seem impossible when attempted alone.

Dialectical Behavior Therapy

Dialectical behavior therapy (DBT) is a comprehensive skill-building framework that addresses problematic coping behaviors like self-harm through compassionate validation. DBT sessions initially focus intensively on teaching mindfulness, distress tolerance, emotion regulation, and interpersonal effectiveness tools, depending on which of these skills is missing (Chapman, 2006).

Therapists actively empathize with overwhelming feelings while guiding alternative outlets like journaling, physical activity, or music for cathartic relief to replace explosions over time. Parent sessions running parallel to the therapy walk through tailored developmental expectations, respecting the unique challenges of each family. The techniques are adjusted to meet each child's needs, teaching them resiliency through consistency. Lifelong skills are developed by the children and their parents.

Incorporating Therapy Techniques at Home

Therapy is not something that you do at the doctor's office and then come home and forget about it. The skills and insights that you learn there will need to be nurtured and practiced at home. Here are some ways parents can incorporate behavioral therapy techniques into their daily home life:

- **Use sticker or star charts:** Use stickers and incentives at home to reward your child when they complete a task they have always struggled with, such as cleaning their room.
- **Role model:** When you use a calm tone and speak positively during disputes, you will motivate your child to do the same. Model emotionally intelligent conflict resolution, and your kids will follow!
- **Schedules:** By having daily written schedules, you can allocate certain times to certain activities like homework, screen time, and dinner. A predictable routine is integral to keeping an explosive child calm and in control.
- **Play "What if" games:** These kinds of games empower kids to articulate constructive solutions, and you get them thinking about problem-solving before the trigger, which prepares them.
- **Safe space:** Set up a space where you can go with your child when they need a break. This is a space where they can have big feelings without judgment before returning to have a peaceful discussion.

Next, let's have a quick look at some exercises and activities that parents can do with their children to help incorporate therapy techniques into their daily routines. You will learn many of these during therapy (and more), and I hate to break it to you, but you will get homework from your therapist!

Journaling

You and your child could keep a separate journal for keeping track of big feelings, explosive episodes, and any private thoughts that you want to come back to later. These can be completely private, or you could use them to share insights together at the end of the week, discussing what went well, praising them for any time they managed to calm themselves, avoid a trigger, or practice any of their new skills.

Feelings Charades

This can be a fun family game—you take turns acting out different emotions for the other to guess. It's a great starting point to talk about big feelings.

Calm Box

Help your kid to create their very own calm box. You can use an old shoe box and decorate it together with paint, glitter, or stickers—just make sure it's personal and you do it together. Then, you can fill the box with small things that help your child to calm down, such as fidget toys, headphones, little magnets, and so on. When your child is beginning to feel overwhelmed or triggered, they can go to their box and play with one of their calming items.

Working With Professionals

In Chapter 2, we discussed the importance of seeking professional help when adjusting your parenting strategies alone is not enough to help tackle explosive behavior. Working with behavioral therapists who implement any of the strategies mentioned earlier is an important step in the right direction when trying to help your child. A well-matched therapist will be able to view the behavior objectively and help to pinpoint triggers, what kinds of skills might need strengthening, and anything you might not be able to see because you are too entrenched in the episodes and feel overwhelmed.

As mentioned, therapy is a collaborative process, and in order for it to be effective, you will have to implement their recommendations at home. If you are more involved and hands-on with the therapist, they will be able to tailor a more personalized treatment plan for you and your child.

Here are some tips for collaborating effectively with the therapist:

- **Open communication:** Make sure you are honest and upfront about behaviors and their impact from the start. Often, parents try to downplay the severity of cases out of shame or a need to protect their child. Honesty from the start will have more effective results.
- **Regular check-ins:** Keep the therapist up to date with techniques you are implementing at home. Let them know if you have made any tweaks, like changing an incentive, or if something isn't working for your family.
- **Be willing to learn/open to different parenting styles:** Starting therapy with your child can sometimes feel uncomfortable. You might feel some resistance to trying out new styles of parenting. That resistance is going to block you from helping your child in the long term, so try to come to this collaboration with an open mind and heart.

By now, you will have a much clearer idea of the synergy between effective communication, understanding discipline, and tailored behavioral techniques. In the next chapter, we're going to take a deeper dive into creating a balanced and stress-free family environment, addressing the dream goals of reduced family stress and balanced family dynamics by building emotional resilience.

CHAPTER 6

BUILDING EMOTIONAL RESILIENCE

At nine years old, Aisha was very possessive of her toys when friends would come over for a playdate. She hovered and tried to dictate how the other child could play or refused to let them touch them at all. She was controlling, and it all inevitably ended in tears and tantrums when Aisha could no longer cope with the stress of it.

Aisha's parents didn't want to stop having playdates, but they knew something had to change. They started having emotional check-ins with Aisha, where they used empathetic listening without judgment to get to the bottom of the meltdowns.

They discovered that Aisha was very protective of her toys because she was terrified of them getting broken. They started teaching Aisha deep breathing exercises and mindfulness to help her find her calm when these worries came. They role-played compromise during play to help her to be more flexible and resilient.

Although Aisha still often worried that her toys might be broken, she discovered the joy that came from compromising during play.

When she started to feel overwhelmed, she would use her deep breathing and mindfulness practice to keep her in control of her own emotions. Aisha and her friends all learned how resilience can transform a child's ability to cope with stress and adversity.

EMOTIONAL INTELLIGENCE IN CHILDREN AND PARENTS

We learned earlier that emotional intelligence refers to the ability to identify and constructively control feelings in oneself and others. This ability involves being able to recognize subjective emotional states through self-awareness, an understanding of how these intuitively shape thinking and interactions, and managing intense reactions via regulation strategies (Psychology Today, n.d.). Emotional intelligence is almost impossible to teach without having an understanding of it yourself first, which is why this chapter is not only about building your child's emotional resilience but your own as well.

Understanding Emotional Intelligence

Emotional intelligence highlights an individual's strengths in understanding emotions and motivations and how these impact behavior and relationships. Experts contend this is equally vital for overall life satisfaction, productivity, and even leadership success (Webb, 2023).

Parents and children with a high level of emotional intelligence are more able to control impulsive reactivity through self-reflection, considerate perspective-taking, and using strategies to ease emotional distress both internally and externally—meaning they are able to emotionally soothe themselves and do not have any huge emotional outbursts or uncontrollable explosive behavior. This creates an environment where everyone feels safe, understood, and dignified.

Emotional intelligence profoundly shapes how children navigate their daily reactions and social interactions, not just at home but at school and beyond. According to researchers, being able to identify and constructively channel their emotions enables children to be more responsible with decision-making, have a more realistic self-appraisal, and to have more resilient responses in the face of conflicts (Webb, 2023).

When children lack or have delayed emotional intelligence skills, they are unable to interpret physiological cues and cannot articulate their feelings. This often shows up as blind reactivity, and kids have little to no behavioral control when they are overcome by frustration, disappointment, or anxiety. This lack of impulse control can have catastrophic effects on their well-being and their ability to form and maintain relationships with others.

According to child psychology experts Daniel Siegel and Tina Payne Bryson, when children can correctly name their emotions, their overwhelming intensity shrinks. This is because "thinking brains" regain their functioning, which is typically drowned out by fight-or-flight limbic reactions. By simply voicing "I see your anger," you can help restore executive functioning within your child and manage their meltdowns easier.

Emotional intelligence has such an important role in behavioral regulation, which is why it is so significant to nurture this skill within yourself and your child. These are skills that will benefit them beyond the four walls of your home and will see them into a much healthier adulthood.

Assessing Emotional Intelligence in Your Child

Now we know what emotional intelligence is and why it's so important to foster this in children, let's take a look at how you can assess your child's current level of emotional intelligence (Kellogg, 2022; Morin, 2021):

Observe their current communication skills:

- Do they confidently initiate conversations?
- OR
- Do they articulate feelings and reactions effectively?

Look for emotional perspective-taking:

- Do they comfort others or consider alternative viewpoints during conflicts?
- OR
- Do they blatantly disregard others' emotional experiences? This can show up as playing too rough or teasing other children.

Watch their distress responses:

- Do they recover from disappointments independently?
- OR
- Do big emotions rapidly escalate into furious screaming, hitting, or withdrawal?

Assess their social adaptability:

- Do they successfully play with children in new environments?
- OR
- Do they play alone and alienate playmates or get distressed?

Understanding your child's baseline emotional skills as they grow supports them long-term.

Once you have investigated your child's emotional intelligence, you can begin to address the areas where your child may be lacking emotional skills.

If a child struggles to express feelings, you can help them by verbally labeling possible emotions during conflicts. This gives them the words they need to develop their understanding and vocabulary—instead of sadness. You might tell them they are feeling disappointed or frustrated, for example.

During meltdowns or conflict, you can model healthy emotional regulation tactics like deep breathing when you are feeling explosive yourself. It's important to also verbalize what you are doing so your child can see and learn from your example: "I'm feeling really frustrated right now, so I'm going to go to the kitchen and do some deep breathing to calm myself down." Then, when you come back, you might say, "I'm feeling calmer now; can we talk about the problem now?"

If your child comes home from school and has had a big argument with a friend at school, you can sit down and role-play with them using stuffed animals or dolls. Try to recreate the argument or a similar one and teach them how to problem-solve during play.

There are also a lot of great books out there for teaching emotional regulation. By choosing stories that focus on empathy, honesty, and self-control, you can instill healthy motivation in your child. You might stop between chapters and discuss what they think might happen next and what the hero should do to resolve the conflict they're in.

Don't forget to praise, praise, praise! Even if they fail to completely regulate themselves, praise them for trying. They need to notice you noticing them to keep them motivated through this journey.

Enhancing Parental Emotional Intelligence

It's not all about your child, remember. In learning about emotional intelligence this far, you may be starting to wonder if you personally have trouble with identifying and controlling your own feelings. If that's the case, or if you just want to work on your own emotional intelligence for personal growth, consider the following exercises (Ackerman, 2019; Millacci, 2022):

- **Journaling:** Starting a journal can feel really daunting, but it doesn't have to be. Simply allocate some time before bed when you can scribble down some things. Once you are used to it, you can be more intentional about what you are writing. Focus on any emotional peaks you had throughout the day—positive and negative. Spend some time reflecting on what you might do differently next time.
- **Mindfulness meditation:** Again, not everyone's cup of tea, but mindfulness meditation can help you to become more aware of your emotions and responses to them. Set yourself regular reminders to stop for five minutes at the same time every day to close your eyes, concentrate on your breathing, and clear your mind. This will also help you to stay calm and composed throughout the day.

- **Reading:** In the same way that you can read with your child to help them learn emotional intelligence, you can do the same. A well-written book will take you through all the emotions of the characters involved. It will help you to empathize and learn how other people react.

There are many other techniques you can draw from to improve your and your child's emotional intelligence. You will find plenty of information available online. The fact that you are willing and want to grow is the most important step here.

STRATEGIES FOR BUILDING RESILIENCE

In Chapter 3, we discussed the importance of resilience in helping families to be more adaptable and to cope better with big feelings and outbursts. Here, we are going to do a deep-dive into strategies and techniques that you can introduce that will help both you and your child to develop your emotional resilience.

Resilience-Building Techniques for Children

Resilience starts in childhood. The foundation that you set for your little one will be carried with them for their entire lives. The following techniques will help you to start that foundation with them (Mayo Clinic Staff, 2020; Mead, 2019):

- **Mindfulness:** You can guide your child in basic meditative breathing or visualization of a peaceful, safe space. Teach them these skills during quiet, peaceful moments and encourage them to use them when they are feeling triggered or explosive. The intention is to access a calming mental state when they are feeling overwhelmed.
- **Positive self-talk:** This doesn't have to be outrageous or over the top. Instead of criticizing themselves, teach them to reframe their thoughts of themselves. Adding the word

"Yet" can be a really powerful technique here. Instead of "I'm not good at this," teach them to say, "I'm not good at this yet." This will help them to have the mentality that they will be able to learn even if they struggle right now.

- **Problem-solving skills:** Often, we find it easier to tell our children what to do for the best, but this can limit them. Even though it might take more time and effort, walk your child through the pros and cons of the situation they are facing and brainstorm solutions with them. This will teach them how to find the answer even if it doesn't come to the right way.

Role of Parents in Building Resilience

Your role in fostering resilience in your children cannot be over-stated here. The more that you model resilience for your child, the easier it will be for them to pick up the skill. Here are some ways parents can play a supportive role in modeling resilience for children:

- **Validation:** Instead of criticizing or judging your child for an explosive episode, use language that reframes their meltdown. For example, instead of, "You are screaming for no reason," you might say, "You had a really hard time leaving the play area today, didn't you?" Make sure you also point out every success that they have with warm, positive praise and validate them that way.
- **Control yourself:** Your own reactions to problems and conflict set the tone for how your child will react to these things in their lives. Make sure you use all the tactics we have discussed this far to breathe through your frustration and tackle problems constructively. Make sure you verbalize your feelings as well: "This is making me feel really frustrated right now."

- **Encouragement:** When you see that your child is having a tough time, you can motivate them by offering support or kind words: "You can do this! Take a minute to calm down and try again."
- **Tell stories:** Kids love listening to their parent's old war stories from their childhoods. Use this opportunity to tell them about times when you struggled to overcome big problems or showed emotional regulation or resilience.

Resilient parenting will offer immediate benefits by helping them to overcome triggers instead of having explosive outbursts. It will also help them to build up their inner strength that they will rely on in their adult lives.

Creating a Resilient Environment at Home

In order to help your child develop their resilience skills, it's important to provide them with a nurturing and stable home environment. Home is the place where they can release all the tension from the school day (which is why they tend to have outbursts immediately after school). So, what can you do to create a resilient environment at home?

First of all, make sure you are showering them with affection, love, and hugs. This doesn't mean clinging onto them all the time; you can show affection by actively listening to them, playing silly games, laughing together, and taking an interest in their interests. The key is to show them that they really matter to you as a person.

You should also allow them space to build their autonomy. Don't do everything for them; let them grow their own competency and tackle tasks alone. It might be easier (and quicker) if you clear out their closet, but let them do it themselves. You could also assign them chores and responsibilities around the house.

This also includes allowing natural consequences to occur. If you wrap your toddler in bubble wrap, they won't learn to stop falling over. Let your older kids make mistakes, and don't protect them from the consequences. For example, you know they've been saving up to buy a game for their console, but then, on impulse, they choose to buy candy and ice cream. It's their money; let them choose how to spend it. However, it means it will take them longer to buy their game.

It's also important to model self-care. When you've all had a long, hard day, snuggle up in your PJs with a hot chocolate and a movie. If you've had a tough day at work, tell them that you are taking some time to yourself and show them what that looks like (bubble bath, going for a jog, coffee with friends).

All of these things will help your child to nurture their resilience skills by providing them with a safe and comforting place to grow.

COPING WITH STRESS AND FRUSTRATION

Emotional intelligence and resilience skills are both key markers in how we all cope with the stress and frustration of everyday life. Let's turn now to explore the different strategies for your children to help them manage the stress that causes their outbursts.

Strategies for Children to Manage Stress

You are never too young to learn stress management techniques such as deep breathing, physical activity, humor, and creative expression. The key is to find an alternative outlet for pent-up feelings and find a way to take control of them instead of letting them control you. Let's take a look at how your child can use these strategies:

Deep Breathing

During stressful moments, deep breathing is a great technique to help your child to center themselves. There are different techniques that you can look into and teach them, which include breath focus, progressive muscle relaxation, or modified lion's breath (Fowler, 2018).

Simple deep breathing involves taking regular pauses for slow, deep belly breaths. This will increase your child's relaxation hormones while lowering their blood pressure and heart rate, both of which are tied to their anxious distress.

Physical Activity

Physical activity is a great way to release any pent-up nervous or frustrated energy. Your little one might like to join a sports club or take up dancing. Even just going to the playground and letting them run around is a great way to get them moving and help them to shift their negative mindset.

Humor

Playing, laughing, and joking all flood the brain with beautiful endorphins, shifting your child's mood and helping them to break free from stress and frustration. Help them to find their smile when they are having a tough time, and in the process, you will be teaching them impactful strategies to shift their own mood.

Creative Expression

Art is motivated by emotions, and it can also be used to shift them. Encourage your child to draw or paint bright and hopeful pictures. Teach them how to journal or get them a craft kit so they can get creative when they need an emotional outlet.

Case Study

The Ali family desperately wanted to help their son Ahmad to learn how to cope with his stress levels in a healthy way. Right now, his explosive tendencies would get the better of him, making the whole family miserable.

They started to teach him deep breathing and meditation skills and took him to an art therapy class they heard about. The combination of these skills and activities helped Ahmad learn how to calm himself down and uplift his mood through art.

Parental Support in Stressful Situations

Your support is even more significant to your child during times of stress and frustration. You are their safe place, and that might mean that you have to bear the brunt of their explosive behavior.

Effectively supporting your child during stressful times means making use of your empathetic listening skills and constructive communication. It means you have to hold off from jumping in with all the solutions every time your child is upset and try to use every challenge that comes up as a learning opportunity and a way to reinforce all of the skills you have started to teach them so far.

According to Mind Tools Content Team (n.d.), empathic listening goes beyond active listening, which we have explored before. Here are a few tips for how to use empathetic listening and constructive communication to support your child during stressful times (Mind Tools Content Team, n.d.):

- Listen patiently without judgment or distractions, allowing children space to air upsets and challenges.
- Mirror back key emotions that you hear using summarizing statements to confirm that you understand the issues.

- Ask clarifying questions that sensitively explore anything that's unclear without making assumptions.
- Attune to their body language and other nonverbal cues that reveal their discomfort.
- Once children feel fully heard, discuss some practical solutions to their problem(s) with them.
- Maintaining confidentiality is really important here to provide a safe outlet for their vulnerabilities and to help them rebuild trust and resilience.

Your support in dealing with stressful situations will help to set the stage for how they cope with stress going forward in their lives.

Preventing Burnout in Parents

Managing explosive behaviors in children can often leave parents feeling burned out, drained, and desperate. It can be a daily onslaught, having to dig deep and find patience and space for our children's emotions. We start to feel exhausted and short-tempered, never far from a tearful explosion ourselves!

There is an old adage that talks about trying to pour from an empty cup—but what does that really mean? It means we spend so much of our time tending to the various needs of our children that we completely neglect our own. Parental burnout is real; it's a "condition in which you're so exhausted that you feel you have nothing left to give" (WebMD Editorial Contributors, n.d.).

The harsh reality is that you cannot be the kind of parent that you want to be if you don't look after yourself, too. Think about that cup again. Imagine that cup is filled with all the patience, calm, self-love, and joy that you want to instill within your child. Every day, you pour them a drink from that cup. You pour, and you pour, and you pour. But you forget to refill the cup. Suddenly, there is no joy, and there is no attentiveness. There's no patience, and there is certainly no calm.

The real question is: How do you fill a cup when you are channeling all your resources into your child, work, housework, meetings, your kid's sports, appointments, and school?

First, you have to realize that burnout doesn't just affect you. This isn't a case of suffering for your child and "taking one for the team" because it will eventually affect them, too. Burned-out parents will be more irritated and stressed; they might distance themselves from their children and can even become violent and neglectful (Abramson, 2021).

It doesn't have to come to that. Let's explore some ways in which you can work on your self-care while still navigating the unique parenting path you have found yourself on.

Tackling Burnout

If you don't make time for your health—both physical and mental —your health will make time for you. If you want to raise a child with empathy, you have to have empathy for yourself, too—and that applies to all children, not just children with OCD, ADHD, and ODD.

If you are feeling burned out, I want you to ask yourself the following questions:

- Are you getting enough sleep?
- Are you eating well?
- Are you keeping on top of your personal hygiene?
- Are you making time for hobbies or interests?

Sleep, food, hygiene, and fun—these four things really can make a great difference to your mental state and, by extension, your parenting. You probably can't make time for a seven-day spa retreat where you can rest, relax, read, and get pampered. That's not always realistic or affordable. However, you can take steps to tackle these four things, which will make a world of difference to your mental health.

Sleep: Sleep might be a real issue in your household. Children with OCD, ADHD, and ODD can struggle with a whole host of sleep-related issues—bedtime anxiety, insomnia, nocturnal awakening, nocturnal activity, early waking, and restless sleep, to name a few (Hvolby, 2015). You might often feel like there's no hope of you ever getting a good night's rest again. I assure you, there are things you can do; the situation is never hopeless. Here are some tips:

- Discuss how you can share the nighttime mental load with your partner or spouse.
- If you no longer live together, come up with a co-parenting plan that gives you the night off every now and then.
- Perhaps the other parent is no longer around at all. In that case, you could reach out to family and friends for some help and respite.
- Work with your pediatrician or specialist and discuss how you can help your child to sleep better.

Food: Sensory problems often go hand-in-hand with food and eating problems. This can be for a variety of reasons: the taste, the mouthfeel, sensitivities of the hands, and so on. Because of this, it can be easy to fall into a routine of "safe" eating. While routine is a fantastic thing for you and your child, continuously eating plain or beige food together because that's all they eat is going to negatively affect your health and energy levels in the long run.

Sometimes, the chaos of life while raising a child with these conditions can be so busy and full-on that you don't take the time to eat at all—do you regularly skip breakfast because the morning is absorbed with simply getting your child to school?

- Think about meal prep. This doesn't have to be anything fancy or have to take up a huge amount of time. When you make a lasagna, consider doubling the ingredients: make two and freeze one.
- Choose fruit. You might often find yourself grabbing an unhealthy snack instead of breakfast. Make a consistent effort to take a banana or an apple instead of that sugar-loaded bar. Over time, consistent effort will become a healthy habit and you'll notice your energy levels improve along with your mental health.

Hygiene: There are many reasons why this task might fall to the bottom of the priority list:

You're just too busy to think about taking time to shower.

- In this case, a schedule is your friend. Plan it into your day and stick to it.

You can't leave your child alone long enough and need someone to watch them while you are out of the room.

- Discuss how you can make this work with the other parent, your family, or your childcare. This might mean getting up slightly earlier and showering while everyone is still in bed.

Your child won't leave you alone long enough to take a shower.

- Some parents take their children in the shower with them. It can be a great bonding experience, depending on their age, or they might just sit nearby and wait for you.
- If that's not for you, remember that routine is great for your child and so are boundaries! It might be hard to establish at first, but if you let your child know that this is

the time you need to shower and that it's non-negotiable, it will eventually become the norm. When our kids see us taking care of ourselves, it also encourages them to do the same. We are their role models, after all.

Fun: What are your hobbies? What are your interests? Perhaps you really struggle to answer that question right now. Often, we can become so absorbed by our parenting journey that we lose bits of ourselves along the way. It doesn't have to be like that, and it's not healthy for you and your child.

Whatever self-care looks like for you, make sure you set aside time for it. In order to be the best parent you can be for your child, you have to look after yourself first!

Clearly, emotional resilience plays a major role in managing explosive behavior—from being able to identify and understand emotions with emotional intelligence to having the ability to get up and try again with resilience. These two things are integral to coping with the stress and frustration that triggers emotional explosions.

Up next, we are going to explore the unique challenges that our explosive children face in educational and social settings and the strategies that we can employ to manage them effectively.

CHAPTER 7

EDUCATIONAL AND SOCIAL CHALLENGES

According to Carpenter et al. (2009), many children with ADHD are disliked within minutes of initial social interaction, which then prevents them from continuing to practice their social skills. They also claim that 50–60% of these children will experience rejection from their peers. These depressing statistics highlight the significance of working on behavioral management techniques in educational environments. Don't worry; there are things we can work on with our little ones to enhance their social skills and peer interactions.

MANAGING EXPLOSIVE CHILDREN AT SCHOOL AND IN SOCIAL SETTINGS

For children who struggle with emotional regulation, school, and playground settings can be extremely triggering for them—especially the unstructured and spontaneous nature of socializing there.

Understanding the Challenges

All children can struggle with socializing, but it can be particularly difficult for explosive children. They may struggle to begin social interactions and to join groups of children when they are already playing. In the same way that they will have explosive outbursts over seemingly unimportant things at home, the same is true at school. When the game or social situation changes unexpectedly, this can be extremely triggering for children who need routine and structure to feel secure and calm.

They may also struggle with the pressures of academic achievement. Fear of failure coupled with being hypersensitive to criticism can result in a whole host of behavior problems at school, which will significantly impact their learning; they might rush through their work or struggle to stay on task. It's possible they could develop an anxiety-inducing sense of perfectionism that keeps them stuck on forming each letter correctly instead of completing the task at hand. While they are being disciplined for their explosive behavior, they will miss many other learning opportunities (Valiente et al., 2011).

Think of the hallways and playground, where noise and bustle could trigger their sensory alarms and send them spiraling into a meltdown. As we know, during a meltdown, explosive children are unreachable; they shout, are inflexible, aggressive (verbally and physically), among a whole host of other things, none of which are healthy or promote friendship and inclusion. "When children have poor self-regulation, school becomes difficult and unpleasant because compliance is challenging, attention control is difficult, and often relationships with teachers are characterized by annoyance and frustration" (Valiente et al., 2011).

In essence, explosive children could be socially excluded both at school and in the big wide world. Quite quickly, they will find themselves isolated. They will no longer be invited for playdates or parties; they will find themselves alone at break time and unable to reach out to their peers. They may also show signs of learning impairments as well.

These social and educational challenges will follow them through the rest of their lives with a rising likelihood of things like divorce and conflict-laden marriages (Caspi et al., 1987).

Strategies for School Success

So, how can we help our explosive children have a better chance at success in school? Let's take a look at some practical tips you can implement right now (Cleare, 2023; Young Minds, n.d.-b):

- Having a visual schedule of their day will help them be prepared and know what to expect.
- A sensory-friendly workstation would also help, for instance, letting them have fidget items at their desk when they feel dysregulated.
- Stick to a reliable morning routine, making sure things like their clothes are sensory-friendly if they have trouble with textures and so on.
- Commit to a safe word or cue that they can give to their teacher, which means they need a strategic brain break or a quick walk outside to prevent a meltdown.
- Make sure teachers are aware and educated about their condition and are checking in with the child regularly to make sure they are keeping up with the workload and not becoming overwhelmed.
- Role-play common or problem social scenarios at home to prepare your child for any difficult situations they might need to navigate alone.

- Speak to parents and invite them for regular playdates to help foster relationships for your child.

When you are collaborating directly with teachers and school staff, make sure that you are all on the same page. The school should be aware of your child's background and common triggers; they will also have training in place for learning how to navigate your child's unique challenges. Later in the chapter, we will discuss support plans that you and the school can implement, which will outline any agreed-upon adaptations for your child. Finally, make sure you are having regular meetings with the school to keep everyone up to date with the child's progress. That way, you can identify any problems early on and help to improve the outcome together.

Navigating Social Settings

Next, let's take a look at some strategies you can implement to help your child to handle social situations:

- **Role model:** This is a powerful way to set your child up for success. Model healthy interactions for them or point out any positive communication you see in movies or TV shows—specifically where you see kindness, inclusion, and overcoming conflict.
- **Reframe:** When they make mistakes during a social interaction, spend time with them discussing what they might do instead next time. Encourage them to figure this out for themselves if they can, or give them multiple options to consider if they struggle with this.
- **Ask questions:** Social interaction can be confusing for all of us. Etiquette and social norms might feel alien to your child, so ask them curious questions about their interactions and see if you can get to the bottom of what they don't understand yet.

Social success really does begin at home. Lead them by modeling how it's done, engaging them in role-playing games where they can practice their social skills, and offering them validation and coaching instead of harsh criticism or judgment.

BEHAVIORAL MANAGEMENT TECHNIQUES IN EDUCATIONAL ENVIRONMENTS

Although school environments can be extremely triggering for explosive children, they can also be a source of help and relief. You should collaborate with the school in adapting behavioral management techniques that are consistent with your efforts at home for maximum effect on your child's development.

Effective Behavioral Interventions at School

You have come to be aware of your child's triggers and precursor behaviors at home, and the teachers and staff should also do the same in order to effectively manage your child's behavior in school effectively. Once they are aware of triggers and precursors, they can begin to implement techniques at school to help your child before, during, and after an outburst.

Here are some generalized tips for the classroom. Make sure you tailor each of these to your child's needs and have regular check-ins with the school:

- **Emotion station:** This is an area where your child can check in with themselves or the teacher when they are feeling emotionally insecure. There might be a wall chart where they can select a visual depiction of how they are feeling.

- **Visual charts:** Having class rules on the walls can remind children of behavioral expectations and help them to toe that line even when they are feeling dysregulated.
- **Reward system:** Having a point or a sticker system provides children with a visual incentive where they can work toward prizes and special treats with positive behavior and emotional regulation.
- **Calm down corner:** In instances when your child becomes dysregulated beyond their control, having a designated area where they can go to calm down will help them to feel secure and regain control quicker. There might be soft pillows, books, or fidgets here for them.
- **Brain breaks:** When your child is feeling dysregulated, unable to concentrate, or out of control, allowing them to go for a walk around the school grounds, run teacher errands to the school office, or take a time-out in the bathroom or closet can give them the much-needed space to calm down and regulate themselves for learning.

Case Study

Describing Alex's behavior in class as "difficult" was an understatement. His teacher wasn't sure what to do for the best. All the children were being disrupted, and it wasn't fair to anyone. After consulting with his parents, they decided to set up an emotion station and a calm-down corner in the classroom—for all the children, not just Alex.

He wasn't sure at first, but Alex was soon a regular in the calm-down corner. The ear defenders and fidget toys were a great distraction when he was starting to feel overwhelmed. It taught him how to remove himself when he felt an explosive episode coming and helped to make the classroom a much calmer environment, improving the learning of all the children.

Parent-Teacher Collaboration

Teachers and school staff are there to help your child to learn. Most likely, your child will not be the first explosive child they would have dealt with, and there will usually be training available to schools to help them to cope with the demands of children with OCD, ODD, and ADHD. A collaborative relationship between parents and teachers is integral to the success of your child in school. Together, you can help to set a secure foundation for your child to grow from.

Parents should provide the school with insights on clinical diagnoses, emotional triggers, family dynamics, and recent setbacks that might need accommodation in school. Meanwhile, teachers will be observing things like peer interactions, any patterns that might be sabotaging the child's learning, and any specific pressures that compromise their emotional regulation. The goal is to set up regular check-ins to keep everyone up to date and keep consistency for the child. This will also help to prevent any serious issues from slipping through the cracks.

Compassionate communication sits at the center of this collaboration; parents should be advocating their child's needs through empathy, not demands or judgment. Being open and honest with the school will help you to develop a customized strategy that reflects the child's capacity and challenges that can be adapted as they grow and develop.

Individualized Education Plans

Individualized Education Programs (IEPs) are federally mandated learning plans custom-tailored to meet explosive students' needs where standardized academic settings fall short. IEP goals target specific behavioral, cognitive, and emotional levels, identified through specialized assessments, where the child needs support.

These personalized interventions secure students "a free and appropriate education" amid once debilitating barriers to educational achievement, with parents working closely alongside clinicians and educators (Child Mind Institute, 2021).

Annual collaborative design sessions allow parents to advocate for individualized accommodations, like if the child needs transition warnings to ease the sensory overload triggered by routine changes. The child will also be able to have modified assignment parameters and testing environments—giving them more time to complete tests if they need it and making sure tests and assignments are accessible to all students.

By law, generated IEPs outline any special instructions and disability supports that the schools should provide students with OCD, ODD, or ADHD where their developmental differences mean they need help to participate. Taking part in ongoing reviews then gauges the effectiveness of the plan and allows you and the school to adjust it as needed.

IEPs essentially allow struggling students equal opportunities to reach their potential in school, which would otherwise be hampered by their conditions and behavior.

In order to obtain an IEP, you will need to submit a written request through your public school district special education department, formally seeking a comprehensive evaluation to determine if an IEP aligns with your child's special needs (King, 2017). Teams will then investigate your child's eligibility and whether any specific learning disabilities require assistance in school.

Once qualified, you will then help to direct the initial planning meetings. Here, you will outline the skill gaps that are interfering with classroom functioning by using assessment data, medical records, and observational anecdotes to convey your child's difficulties. Together, IEP teams will then select customized interventions to address hurdles, like implementing transitional warnings to prevent sensory overload when routines abruptly change or allowing extra time for tests.

Optimizing IEP effectiveness means continually tracking the plan's implementation and progress toward the written goals and requesting adjustments or expanded special services as needed. Annually updating the IEP to match your child's evolving needs is imperative, and it also ensures schools uphold their legal mandate, securing your explosive child's ongoing academic growth.

ENHANCING SOCIAL SKILLS AND PEER INTERACTIONS

Just because your child struggles with peer interactions right now does not mean they always will. In this section, we are going to take a look at how you can teach your child social skills, facilitate positive peer interactions, and how to handle bullying and exclusion.

Teaching Social Skills

Many of the skills and learning we have discussed so far will contribute massively toward teaching your child social skills. Think of things like role-playing with them, where you can teach them to share, compromise, and handle disappointment. Also, watching films or reading books and pointing out positive examples is great for teaching them about inclusion and integrity. Helping them to find role models in real life can also be useful for explosive children; it might be an older sibling or a cousin, perhaps someone at school they could buddy up with who they can observe and model after.

Other than looking for role models and role-playing, there are some activities and games that you can do with your child that encourage social skill development (Positive Action Staff, 2020):

- **Emotion charades:** Just as you would play normal charades, you write down the different emotions and put them in a hat. Take it in turns to choose an emotion and act it out. Your child will then need to use and read body language and facial expressions to win the game, a skill that they can use in real-life social scenarios.
- **Staring contest:** Eye contact can be really tough for explosive children, but it's also important during social interaction, so this is a great activity to get them practicing in a low-pressure, fun way.
- **Simon says:** This game is lots of fun and great for teaching children self-control and working on their listening skills. In this game, you are Simon, and you give the child actions to do, but they should only do the action if you say, "Simon says..." For example, when you say, "Simon says... jump up and down," they must follow the directive. If you simply say, "Spin around" without "Simon says," they shouldn't spin around.

There are many other activities and games you can play to encourage the development of social skills. Things as simple as building a tower together is great for collaboration. Consider different board games or even online games with friends where they have to communicate and collaborate to win. Sports are also great for team building.

Facilitating Positive Peer Interactions

You should have noticed by now that parents play a pivotal role in building and reinforcing their children's social and interaction skills. Not just through directly teaching them, but through modeling and play, you set their foundation.

You can go a step further than that by being more than their foundation; you can continually encourage their growth. If you shower them with praise after a positive interaction or even attempts at an interaction, you will reinforce their initiative and courage. Notice the small steps that they take; if you know your child struggles to join in with others and you notice them asking to play at the playground, then congratulate them later on.

Some children struggle to understand things like sarcasm or disinterest. In this case, you can discuss body language and tone of voice with them. Demonstrate examples so they understand or notice it in future interactions.

As a parent, there are many things you can do to create opportunities for positive peer engagement. If you see other children looking isolated or left out, encourage your child to invite them to play; teach them inclusion, and they will teach others. Host get-togethers or play dates regularly with two or three children with similar interests. If they are older, help your child to plan study groups. Enrolling them in clubs or sports that are of interest to your child is also a great way to foster friendships and teamwork.

Handling Bullying and Exclusion

As much as victimization shouldn't exist, unfortunately, it does. We opened this chapter with the fact that many children with ADHD are disliked within minutes of initial social interaction, which paves the way for exclusion and even bullying.

Bullies are likely to target children who are more vulnerable due to their learning difficulties, stimming or impulsive behaviors, and with little to no social skills, an explosive child might even misinterpret the signs of bullying as playfulness or may not know how to deal with being excluded by their peers.

If your child comes to you and you suspect they may be experiencing bullying or social exclusion, there are some strategies you can implement to support them:

- **Validate, validate, validate:** We've said it before; let's say it again: Validate how your child is feeling. Help them to label emotions like shame and humiliation and give them the words for what is happening to them. Children who lack social and emotional awareness may not be able to report bullying because they can't put into words what is happening and what they are feeling. By validating them, you can give them the courage to report the incident and speak out against bullies who might claim to have done nothing wrong.
- **Report incidents:** This leads us to the second point. Make sure you are communicating with the school. Encourage your child to speak to teachers and speak to them yourself, too.
- **Role-play again:** Another great use for role-playing with your child is to teach them how to respond and react to bullies. Role-play a scene with dolls or soft toys and demonstrate how to advocate for themselves and seek help from teachers when necessary.
- **Build friendships:** If your child is struggling with being included, follow some of the tips mentioned in the previous section: host playdates or get-togethers, sign them up for sports or clubs, and encourage them to foster friendships.

As we have seen, it is so important to address your child's educational and social challenges, and there are ways you can collaborate with the school to help offer them a well-rounded experience despite their challenges. Address any concerns around bullying or social exclusion as they come up, and spend time playing games and teaching your child social skills to see them through their school experience. You can even assist your child in creating and building friendships.

In the next chapter, we're going to look closely at lifestyle and environmental factors, providing insights into developing effective communication strategies that foster understanding and cooperation within the family and with external support systems.

CHAPTER 8

LIFESTYLE AND ENVIRONMENTAL FACTORS

The environment itself will teach the child, if every error he makes is manifest to him, without the intervention of a parent of teacher, who should remain a quiet observer of all that happens.

— MARIA MONTESSORI

This powerful quote by Maria Montessori sets the stage for understanding how a child's immediate environment plays a crucial role in their development, especially for children with behavioral challenges. A child's home environment, their routines, and even their sleep and eating habits can have a tremendous impact on their behavior—both positively and negatively.

IMPORTANCE OF SLEEP AND DIET

First, let's think about the effect that sleep and diet can have on emotional regulation and behavioral issues. "In studies with children and adolescents, it was found that sleep deprivation increased depression, confusion, and anger, as well as feelings of frustration and irritability/aggression" (Vandekerckhove & Wang, 2017, p. 3). So, you can imagine how this would affect a child who already has explosive tendencies.

The Impact of Sleep on Behavior

For everyone, a lack of sleep and adequate rest can leave us feeling grumpy and unable to concentrate well. According to Better Health Channel (2022), it can also have an impact on our judgment and coordination, "affecting how we feel, think, work, learn, and get along with other people."

Daytime behaviors, such as emotional regulation, focus, and impulse control, are all affected by inadequate sleep. Explosive children will struggle more than usual with their self-control and regulation abilities, affecting their problem-solving and stress-management skills. Therefore, it's important to ensure that your explosive child is getting as much restful sleep as possible. Let's take a look at some sleep hygiene practices tailored for explosive children (Centers for Disease Control and Prevention, 2022; Suni, 2022; Your Headspace Mindfulness & Meditation Experts, n.d.):

- Maintain firm, consistent bedtimes and wake times, including at the weekends. This will help to set a foundation for your child's natural body rhythms.
- Make sure you allow time to unwind before bed. You could offer a warm bath or read with your child to ease the transition toward them feeling sleepy.
- No screens before bed. This should be a hard and fast rule for 1–2 hours before bed. Screens cause dopamine and cortisol activity, which keeps brains (both adult and child) wired and unable to sleep.

- You could consider using some calming essential oils like lavender and practice guided meditation with your child to help them ease any racing thoughts they might have.
- Create a cozy, cool, tranquil bedroom environment reserved just for sleeping and storytelling. Having a TV or a wall full of stimulating toys is going to prevent sleep and keep their brains awake.
- You could try using weighted blankets or give your child a relaxing massage on their legs and arms to help with any physical restlessness.
- Having a chart or a color-coded wall clock to signal daytime activities and bedtime routines can be a great visual aid for your child to understand what things should happen and when.
- It's also important to rule out any medical or undiagnosed conditions like sleep apnea or reflux that might be causing sleep disruption.

Getting on top of your child's sleep hygiene can be instrumental in improving challenging explosive behavior. Remember, routine is key, and bedtime should not be stressful or stimulating. As soon as you start getting frustrated, your child will, too. So stay calm, even if their behavior is testing your limits. Take it easy and implement the tips above. You'll be surprised at the difference in your child when their sleep is under control.

Case Study

Farrah had never slept through the night. Not ever. As a baby, she had terrible reflux that kept her awake throughout the night. She grew out of the reflux, but she still didn't sleep. Her parents were always exhausted after work, so they preferred to spend the evenings watching TV with Farrah before bed. When she turned six with no sign of her sleep improving, her parents sought help.

They took on board the recommendations and started implementing a different evening routine: the TV went off at 6 p.m., and they gave Farrah a bath instead. They bought a selection of books and would lay in bed with her and read after bath time, and tucked her in with a weighted blanket at the same time every night. Farrah took to the new routine right away, and everyone got more rest because of it.

Diet and Behavioral Health

Next, we're going to consider the role of diet in your child's explosive behavior. If you are being truly honest with yourself right now, how balanced is your child's diet? Are they eating enough of the necessary food groups? How is their sugar intake?

Nutritional research has shown direct links between diet and children's abilities to regulate their behavior (Selhub, 2022). Diets that include high-sugar foods like refined carbohydrates can create blood sugar spikes and crashes. This leaves children struggling with their impulse control and with calming down as their energy levels override their cognitive ability (Micanti et al., 2018). Deficiencies in supplements like Omega oils are also associated with worsened focus, aggression control, and general moods.

Common additives or compounds in produce may also generate sensory sensitivity, which can trigger meltdowns in explosive children and elimination diets have been shown to alleviate ADHD and autism outbursts (Barnhill et al., 2018). Overall, it is clear that poor nutrition is likely going to put a strain on your child's regulation abilities.

The idea of improving your child's diet might seem simple, but it can be challenging—especially if your child struggles with sensory problems related to food. Here are some dietary guidelines that will help you to support your child's mental and emotional health; these are simply guidelines, so remember to adapt your strategy based on your child's individual needs (Mental Health Foundation, 2022; Micanti et al., 2018; Selhub, 2022):

- Consistent meal and snack times will help to stabilize your child's blood sugar and energy levels. You may have already noticed that hunger can be a trigger for your child, so do your best to get ahead of those meltdowns.
- Staying hydrated is another important factor here. Offer water with every meal, and make sure a drink is always available. For younger children, that might mean having a sippy cup at hand. For older children, that means making sure cups are within reach, and they can access fresh water when they want it. You may have to prompt them until they get used to their body signal. Adequate hydration will support their concentration skills as well as keep them regulated.
- Make sure that their diet includes a healthy balance of essential fatty acids like Omega oils. This will regulate their neurotransmitters and reduce any inflammation that might be tied to poor mental health.
- Increase their fruit, vegetable, and fiber intake, which all provide critical vitamins and minerals to nourish brain function. To do this, you can always have the fruit bowl full and available and always include vegetable sides with their meals.
- It's also a great idea to incorporate lean proteins with each meal to supply key amino acid building blocks.
- You might also consider eliminating common allergenic foods like dairy, eggs, or gluten. There is some discussion that they may generate brain fog or outbursts in sensitive children. It's best to tailor this to the needs of your child, though.

- Reducing their intake of heavily processed items should be high on your list of things to do. Added sugar can contribute to mood swings and exhaust your child's self-discipline reserves.
- Consider including some probiotic foods in their diet, benefiting gut-brain connections. You can add things like yogurt, kefir, and kimchi, all of which aid healthy digestion and immunity resilience.

These things are not only good for your child's body, but they will also contribute to their well-being. We all need to acknowledge the link between a healthy body and a healthy mind—the two are inextricably linked, and together, they make up the whole person.

Identifying and Managing Food Sensitivities

Although the impact of food sensitivities remains under-recognized, research increasingly highlights the diet's influence on mental health (Grajek et al., 2022). This goes beyond nutritional deficiencies; it's possible to have sensitivities to compounds in foods, and this may generate inflammation and test the coping capacities of explosive children.

Think for a moment about how an upset stomach impacts *your* mood and coping capacity. Foods that trigger bloating or reflux can easily overwhelm the nervous system of your explosive little one in the same way they would for you. Another symptom of food sensitivities can be brain fog (Campos, 2020). This would severely impact the child's already strained school experience, so it's something to look into.

There is also evidence that suggests food dyes and flavor enhancers can increase hyperactive behavior in all children, not just those with ADHD, OCD, and ODD (WebMD Editorial Contributors, 2008). Even excessive amounts of sugar can have an impact on the energy and hyperactivity levels of children due to the blood sugar spike it causes. Some children can be more sensitive to dyes and sugar than others; it's a good idea to begin a food diary if you suspect your child might have any kind of food sensitivity. This would involve writing down everything your child eats over the period of a week and also tracking any explosive or negative behavior around the same time.

Take a look at the sample food diary below. Use this to track your child's food intake, and if you notice a common trigger, try an elimination diet to see if that has any effect on their behavior.

Date	Foods eaten (meals and snacks)	Behavior noticed
Monday	Breakfast: Snack: Lunch: Snack: Dinner:	Energy: Mood: Focus: Explosive episodes:
Tuesday		
Wednesday		
Thursday		
Friday		
Saturday		

CREATING A SUPPORTIVE HOME ENVIRONMENT

Your child's home environment is made up of a few factors: their physical environment, their emotional environment, and who they live with. These three things can have an influence on your child's behavior, which means you can get ahead and use them to your advantage now.

Physical Environment and Its Influence

We've already discussed the school environment and how a cluttered, loud, or cramped space might impact your child's learning and regulation. The same is true at home. A chaotic and overstimulating space is going to contribute to your child's explosive behavior. However, this means that the opposite is also true; if you can create a home environment where your child feels calm and at ease, then this can help them with their emotional regulation.

That is not to say that you now have to make sure your home is spotless and perfectly organized every single day. Instead, focus on making sure your child's space is organized and their things are accessible. Make sure the layout of the furniture is intuitive so they can move around freely without feeling cramped or overwhelmed.

Things you should consider to create a sensory-friendly home environment include:

- **Noise levels:** Make sure things like the TV or radio are at a comfortable level.
- **Lighting:** Think about using the mellow lighting of lamps rather than harsh overheads, which can be overstimulating.
- **Calm corner:** Set up a calm corner filled with blankets, books, and fidgets. Make this a peaceful space for them.
- **Visual cues:** Having bedtime or morning routines pinned up on a laminated sheet does wonders for children who struggle with routine or struggle remembering what to do. Having visual cues strategically placed prevents meltdowns before they happen by providing the child with the solution to their problem before it even happens.

Making these small adjustments (and others tailored to your child's needs) will help the whole family enjoy a much more relaxed and calm home environment with fewer explosive outbursts.

Emotional Environment

Research highlights that stable, nurturing home environments provide the emotional security that enables children to develop their self-regulation skills. Co-regulation is a key aspect in creating this kind of home environment. It is an emotional regulation process between children and caregivers that relies on the emotional atmosphere being consistently calm, empathetic, and encouraging (Rosanbalm & Murray, 2017).

When parents reactively escalate during interactions and display anger or criticism, then the children will follow and mimic this. They will then not learn the skills they need or learn to cooperate. However, when parents can model self-control by being patient, soothing, and regulated even when the child is pushing them, their child will learn to mirror that and use those same skills when they are feeling pushed to their limits.

De-escalation doesn't always mean being patient in the moment; it can also involve excusing yourself from the confrontation so you can calm down—as long as it is safe to do so. Then, when you return, you show your child that you have self-regulated and are ready to problem-solve with them positively. This teaches them that everyone experiences these same emotions and that taking yourself away and calming down will lead to better outcomes.

Co-regulation means nurturing emotional stability and will teach your child that you will face challenges compassionately together.

Here are some tips you can implement to maintain calm and emotional consistency (Kinne, 2022; Lovevery, 2022):

- Try not to react immediately when your child is exhibiting explosive behavior.
- Pay attention to your body signals—are you stiff with clenched fists and a furrowed brow?

- Practice deep breathing and visualize the tension leaving your body.
- Steer clear of yelling, criticism, and judgment—offer acknowledgment and validation instead.
- Sometimes, talking only makes the situation worse. You could try sitting with your child, offering them a hug, or just placing a hand on their leg or shoulder until they are ready to talk. Physical contact shows them that you care and are there for them when they are ready.
- Apologize when you do blow up. It's natural, and we all have bad days; the key thing here is to apologize if you have lost your temper or spoken to your child in a way you wish you hadn't.

Consistency is absolutely key when it comes to creating a nurturing emotional environment. Your child will notice your effort, and they will mirror your actions through co-regulation.

Involving Siblings in Creating a Supportive Environment

Often, the home environment isn't simply about what the parents do; siblings also have a role in shaping this environment. Research shows that reciprocal sibling relationships that are characterized by mutual support, empathy, and constructive conflict resolution have a profound impact on children's regulation abilities (Paley & Hajal, 2022). Your explosive child has the opportunity to learn from their siblings' modeled behavior, and they can also offer co-regulation.

However, in families where siblings show frequent hostility and aggression, it becomes extremely important for parents and caregivers to step in before resentment takes root. As the caregiver, you also must not show any preferential treatment during disagreements and help both children to calm down.

There are many ways in which you can involve siblings positively without burdening them or encouraging resentment. You might ask for everyone's input when it comes to days out, vacations, or even redecorating, helping everyone to feel included and feel like their opinion matters. You can help them work on their cooperation skills by giving them shared chores or shared rewards for completing their chores. Help the children to nurture their relationship with one another through shared activities or crafts. When it comes to conflict, it's best not to force children to apologize but instead encourage them to compromise and problem-solve together.

The key is to uplift the children's strengths and reframe any differences. Trust them, empathize with them, and encourage team-building games and activities. Sibling relationships can be rewarding and nurturing for everyone.

THE ROLE OF ROUTINE AND STRUCTURE

Finally, we've arrived at a deeper discussion of routines and structure, a point we have touched on many times throughout the book. Here, we will discuss how to establish effective routines, how we can implement flexibility through this structure, and finally, some tips for transitioning between activities.

Establishing Effective Routines

Often, children with ADHD, OCD, or ODD need set routines in order to keep them emotionally regulated. Sometimes, new activities can be overwhelming or overstimulating, and routine can help to ground explosive children during these times (Turner, 2023). Explosive children can also struggle with remembering what is expected of them every day (brushing their teeth and hair, for example), and having an established routine helps them to remember and attend to those things.

Routines provide stability and predictability for explosive children; it will help them with their time management, reduce stress, and help regulate their circadian rhythm (Koseva, 2023). Therefore, establishing an effective routine is crucial to helping them stay calm and regulated, and they will grow more confident and secure. It also gives them a sense of control over their lives, which can be a huge trigger for explosive behavior.

In order to create and maintain effective routines, you should always take your child's preference into consideration. For example, if your child prefers to brush their teeth before they get dressed, let that be the set order of things in the morning. The priority is getting both tasks done, regardless of the order in which they are done. Having a visual board where your child can check in on themselves throughout the day can really help to build their independence and confidence. But make sure you aren't scheduling every block of time; leave windows for unpredictability, like family night. Fun is planned, but the game, movie, or activity is undecided. Sometimes, setting digital reminders or alarms can be helpful in transitioning between activities. Overall, make sure that you are praising your child's dedication and cooperation at every turn.

Flexibility Within Structure

While routine can be extremely important for an explosive child's well-being, it's also important to balance a degree of flexibility with consistency. In the big wide world, not everything always goes to plan. So, in order for them to build resilience, it's important to also teach them about flexibility. As the parents of explosive children, it's also vital for us to understand that we are also going to have to be flexible with the routines we put in place in order to accommodate the sometimes unpredictable nature of our explosive children.

So, how can we balance the need for structure with the need for flexibility?

- Build routines that have backup plans. For example, most days, you walk to school. On days when you are running late, you take the car.
- Put together a sensory travel kit that stays in the car or comes with you when you are out and about. Make sure you have things like ear defenders and fidget toys at hand for when the unexpected happens.
- Transitions can be tough, so prepare your kid by giving warnings every five minutes leading up to the change in activity. For example, when you are planning to leave the playground, warn them 15 minutes before and then every 5 minutes until it's time to leave.
- Most importantly, ask your child's opinion or perspective when routines need to be adjusted. Giving them a chance to have an input helps prevent them from feeling like the situation is out of their control.

The key to including flexibility in structure lies in first acknowledging that your child has their own preferences and being prepared for things to go off the plan every now and then. If you remain calm and navigate through change smoothly, your child will learn from that.

Transitioning Between Activities

As mentioned above, transitions can be difficult for explosive children. Often, they don't have the skills to quickly jump from one task to the next and need a little bit more help from us.

First off, it's important to acknowledge if your child struggles with this. Sometimes, parents will try to brush it off in the hopes that if they are nonchalant, their child will be, too. This will only make them frustrated and unable to vocalize it. Get down to your child's level and verbalize how they are feeling, "You don't want to leave the playground, do you?"

Don't forget to give them warnings leading up to the transition so they can get used to the idea. You can also give them a transitional bridge to help them move from one activity to the next. For example, whenever it's time to tidy up, sing a tidy-up song.

Your visual boards can also be a big help here when transitioning. Instead of telling your child what they have to do next, ask them to check the board and see what activity is next—"Is it time for dinner, or do we have to do your homework next?"

Finally, as always, role-playing is your friend here, too. This is especially important for the bigger transitions, like starting or changing schools or moving house. You can help them to understand what to expect through play.

While environmental factors are crucial to our explosive children's well-being, sometimes, advanced strategies are necessary as well. In the next chapter, we will delve into complex cases and advanced techniques for dealing with outbursts on the more extreme end of the scale.

CHAPTER 9

ADVANCED STRATEGIES AND TECHNIQUES

S tudies show that "approximately 15% of children with behavioral disorders present cases that are complex and diffi- cult to manage with standard approaches" (Ogundele, 2018). This statistic emphasizes the need for advanced strategies for children who won't necessarily respond to all the advice we have discussed so far.

ADDRESSING COMPLEX CASES AND SEVERE OUTBURSTS

Sometimes, explosive behavior goes beyond what we can cope with as parents, making us feel as though we are on the edge of a break- down ourselves. We might find ourselves wondering what we did so wrong on our parenting journey or if there is anything else going on beyond our children's diagnosis.

Understanding Complex Cases

Complex cases of explosive behavior go beyond the usual impulsive, aggressive tantrums, screaming, and violence that we have discussed thus far. According to Synapse (n.d.), complex and challenging behaviors also include self-injury, hyper-sexuality, and property destruction.

It's important to take a multidisciplinary approach to these kinds of behaviors, and this means drawing on different strategies, techniques, and even professional help when necessary to tackle the behavior and ensure safety above all.

Techniques for Managing Severe Outbursts

When dealing with severe outbursts, it's important to make sure everyone is safe as your first priority. If the child is causing self-injury or injury to others, use the least amount of control necessary to make sure they aren't continuing to do so. This might mean removing any dangerous items immediately or removing the other person/child from the room entirely to keep them safe from harm from the outburst. If you are somewhere public, try to find a secluded area where you can take your child for some privacy.

If they are open to physical contact, a hug or a touch on their arm might help to ground and calm them down. If they are not open to it, simply being in the room and remaining calm might be a comfort to them. For some children, it might be overwhelming if you try to talk to them now, but for others, they may find it helpful if you were to talk to them in soothing, calming tones—this really depends on the needs of your child.

Make sure that communication after this is clear and direct once they are ready. Reiterate boundaries and firm rules (like: "It's okay to be frustrated, but it is not okay to hurt your brother). Validate their feelings and use the strategies that we have discussed so far in this book when the child is calm enough for them to be effective.

Remember, when your child is at the height of emotional flooding, they can't hear or understand reasoning. Help them to calm down and self-regulate before you think about opening a dialogue about the trigger or the behavior.

Case Study

Carlos was diagnosed with multiple behavioral disorders by the time he was ten years old. Home was more like a war zone than anything. His parents struggled to get him into school, and when he was there, he was a ticking time bomb. With the help of the school, Carlos' parents sought professional help. He began behavioral therapy and medication as a dual approach to help with his violent explosions. The medication helped to calm him and improve his focus. He was finally able to learn behavior management techniques with the help of this therapist, and things began to rapidly improve for the family.

When to Seek Professional Help

Children from the ages of two to seven will have regular tantrums, and they are developmentally appropriate. If these emotional outbursts continue beyond the age of seven, that is a sign that something else might be going on. As they get older and physically bigger and stronger, outbursts can be more difficult and even dangerous to the child and those around them.

If you see any of the following indicators, consider seeking professional intervention for your child:

- Inconsolable self-harming behaviors like head-banging
- Recurring physical aggression that causes injury to themselves or others

- Consistent public outbursts despite strategies being implemented at home and school
- The whole family's schedules, plans, and lifestyle revolve around avoiding outbursts

If professional support becomes necessary, you should speak to your medical provider first. Your child's pediatrician will be able to refer them for other services such as child psychologists, psychiatrists, behavioral therapists, or neuropsychologists.

It's important at this point to do your research to determine which professional or service might be right for you and your child based on the behavior they are displaying. Discuss your options with your pediatrician, and they will be able to guide you in making a decision. You can refer back to the list of professionals in Chapter 2 to help you.

ADDITIONAL THERAPY TECHNIQUES AND INTERVENTIONS

Among your options for therapy and intervention are things like art therapy, play therapy, and animal-assisted therapy. These can be utilized alongside traditional treatments like medication and behavioral therapy.

Innovative Therapy Options

The following techniques may be less conventional, but they are growing in popularity among mental health professionals.

Art Therapy

According to Psychology.org Staff (2023), studies have shown that art therapy can help those with depression, anxiety, mood-related disorders, trauma, and PTSD. Because our explosive children struggle to express their emotions, an artistic outlet might be hugely beneficial to them, whether that be through painting, music, or dance.

Play Therapy

An excellent resource for children, play therapy allows children to explore their feelings without having to use words (Play Therapy UK, 2021). It's all child-led, and it can help to bring issues to the surface, such as anxiety and trauma. The play includes anything from puppets (think about the role-playing we've discussed already) to playing with sand, painting, and physical movement.

Animal-Assisted Therapy

During this therapy, the child would interact with an animal alongside the therapist—the animal might be a cat, a dog, a fish, a bird, or anything! (Urwin & Holroyd, n.d.). This can also help with mood disorders and trauma, and it involves general contact with the animal. The therapy is modified according to the animal and how the child is engaging with it.

These kinds of therapies can complement traditional approaches, allowing the child to explore their emotions in new and exciting ways. It can help them to have an outlet for feelings that they simply don't have the words for yet, which can then be used in traditional therapy to develop strategies specifically tailored for the child and their needs.

The Role of Medication

The reaction to medicating a child with ADHD, OCD, or ODD is generally mixed. Some people are against it, while others will advocate for it. It's important to weigh up both the pros and the cons as you would with any medication need. Things to consider are when symptoms are outside of what the family can manage, if the child is struggling with their mental health and having dangerous or suicidal thoughts, and if the child has requested to try medication to help them focus at school. It's a decision for the family to make.

Medication can also be vitamins and holistic remedies. It might be worth trialing these first before going to the over-the-counter pharmacy or prescribed medication.

ADHD medication targets the brain chemicals known as dopamine and norepinephrine, which affect attention and concentration (Kids Health, n.d.). Children with ODD might be prescribed stimulant medication or antipsychotics in tougher cases (Lovering, 2021). For OCD, medications that increase serotonin are prescribed, selective serotonin reuptake inhibitors (SSRIs) (Mind, 2019).

It's important to remember here that if you choose to medicate your child, it does not have to be forever. It can help you to navigate the tough times and give you the opportunity to teach them the much-needed skills we have discussed earlier in the book. It can be useful when used in conjunction with other therapies, helping them to develop strategies that will carry them through once they are off medication again.

Case Study

Ian was diagnosed when he was seven. His middle school education was tough, and he could often be found in the supply closet doing push-ups against the shelving units to expend his restless energy. By the time he reached high school, he decided he wanted to be more present in class. At an appointment with his pediatrician, he asked if he could try medication. He told the doctor about how he struggles to get to school on time, his outbursts in class, and his struggles with maintaining friendships. "I don't want to get sent to the principal's office anymore," he said quietly.

The following week, Ian had his medication, and he was ready to go to school. His parents and teachers all reported instant results. He wasn't late for school anymore, homework was getting done on time and without a fuss, and he was finally able to sit through all his lessons during the school day without needing to go for a walk or a stretch.

Parent Training and Support

Attempting to manage the most severe behavioral struggles alone or as a family can quickly drain any parent past empty. This doesn't have to be a solo journey. Outside of traditional support like therapists and medication, you can reach for assistance as a parent.

First off, consider joining support groups of parents in the same or similar positions as you. You will find support and camaraderie there as well as experience, wisdom, and advice that you might not find online or in a book. Connection and friendship can help you from feeling so alone and isolated during the hardest times.

You can also consider taking part in evidence-based parenting training such as parent management training (PMT) or the Positive Parenting Program (Triple P) (Fongaro et al., 2022; Miller, 2016). These kinds of programs help parents build their own emotional regulation and de-escalation abilities, teaching skills to help deal with explosive behavior. Here, you will find self-confidence and a deeper, practical understanding of the techniques and skills we have discussed throughout the book so far.

Resources and Programs for Parents

Support groups:

- CHADD groups for ADHD parenting support
- Local or online meetup groups for neurodiverse parenting advice

Intervention programs:

- Triple P Positive Parenting Program (all ages)
- Parent-Child Interaction Therapy (ages 2–7)
- The Incredible Years (ages 0–12)
- Parent Management Training (ages 3–13)

Online parent training:

- Centers for Disease Control and Prevention Parent Training Modules
- The Inner Challenge 30-Day Parenting Challenge

Advocacy organizations:

- Federation of Families for Children's Mental Health
- CHADD

There are so many resources available that can help you to boost your parenting confidence, knowledge, and practical skills. Don't ever be afraid or ashamed to reach out.

PREDICTING AND PREVENTING ERUPTIONS

Catching an explosion before it happens will always be the best way to deal with it. As we discussed earlier in the book, the best way to do this is to learn how to recognize the early warning signs that signal an emotional eruption is coming.

Recognizing Early Warning Signs

Here, we're going to look at the S.E.A.T. framework for how to spot the early signs of an impending outburst (O'Neal et al., 2019):

S—Sensory

Children might begin to use self-stimulating behaviors or "stims" to soothe themselves and relieve stress (National Autistic Society, 2020). Stimming behavior can be a sign that the child is feeling anxious, uncertain, or distressed. Keep an eye out for frequent rocking, hand flapping, jumping, or any repetitive behavior. Remember that these behaviors reflect internal tension spikes and are not deliberate defiance. If you notice your child displaying any stimming behavior, it's best to accommodate them to help prevent a total system overload next.

E—Escape

You might notice that they are "running away" from a demand that is placed on them. This doesn't necessarily mean physically running away; it simply means there is clear avoidance behavior. For example, the parent or caregiver tells the child to go clean their room, and the child starts having a tantrum. Their behavior signals that they do not want to do the chores. Often, parents will feel the need to take control of the situation here and force the issue. Just because your child isn't able to do the chore right now doesn't mean they won't be able to do it later on when they are feeling more regulated and in control. This is really a case of picking your battles sometimes. Take a break and come back to the chore later on. You don't lose parenting points if your kid doesn't clean their room right away, but by giving them the chance to regulate and come back, you will be nurturing your bond with them, their emotional regulation skills, and consistency.

A—Attention

Some of the signs that children are looking for attention include suddenly acting silly or telling jokes, interrupting, minor misbehaviors, or requesting help with a task they can do themselves. By noticing these bids for attention, you can meet their need for attention and prevent an outburst from bubbling up. They might just want a quick hug or acknowledgment. Even if you are busy, take a moment to notice them. If you need to ask them to wait while you finish a task, then make sure you stick to the deadline you set. If you say, "I'll be with you when I finish the dishes," then go to them when you finish instead of starting another chore while they are distracted. Teach them that they can trust you, and they will learn to be patient, their attention needs will be met, and their outbursts will be avoided.

T—Tangible

Sometimes, children will have an immediate "want." This could be anything tangible, from food to an item they see in the store. This can quickly escalate into an emotional explosion when the answer is going to be, "No." It might be reasonable to give in to their request —they really want an ice cream on a hot day as you pass the ice cream store and you decide it would be a nice treat. Other times, it might be unreasonable, for example, if they suddenly want to do arts and crafts but you have to leave for school in five minutes. Remember, empathy and validation come first. Remind yourself that their intention is not to make you late or to have a meltdown, even if your own frustration tried to trick you into thinking that way. An outright "No" will trigger an eruption. Instead, ask them curious questions about why they want to do this activity or have this item right now. Then, brainstorm a solution with them; make a plan for when they can do their arts and crafts and follow through —even if they forget. When you remind them after school that they have plans, they will be grateful, and it will strengthen the trust and bond between you for the next time this kind of meltdown is looming.

Proactive Strategies to Prevent Outbursts

Being proactive against explosive behavior can feel liberating as a parent. Catching and redirecting behavior before it happens benefits the whole family. Let's look at some strategies that you can employ to prevent behavioral eruptions:

- **Morning regulation rituals:** Begin your day with calming music, breathing exercises, or petting animals. Choose activities that your child finds the most calming and add them to your morning routine. This way, you can establish emotional baselines for the day.
- **Audit triggers:** Spend some time identifying your child's triggers at home and discuss possible solutions with them. If they find mealtimes to be hectic and overwhelming, consider staggering everyone's breakfast time, for example. You might get your explosive child up half an hour before everyone else, and they can eat in peace before everyone else starts bustling around the kitchen.
- **Role-playing triggers:** If there is something that consistently triggers your child but you can't always avoid it, then use your role-playing skills to help build their resilience to it. If your child regularly feels overwhelmed in the classroom, you can role-play and teach them how to use coping mechanisms, relaxation techniques, and to ask for help when they need it.
- **Focus on compassionate communication:** Invest some consistent family time to share gratitude and appreciation for one another. This is a great way to have meaningful dialogue over dinner—you can discuss mistakes and unpack any conflicts that might be happening within the family. Emphasize compassion, forgiveness, and, most importantly, the value of the relationships.

- **Preempt sensory overload:** When you begin to notice the signs that your child is pending an eruption, you can intervene and redirect them before it happens. Make sensory adaption toolkits (sunglasses, headphones, weighted blankets, etc.) and leave them freely available to your child to help prevent outbursts.

Building Resilience and Coping Skills

In Chapter 6, we devoted some time to learning how to teach explosive children resilience and coping skills. Now, it's time to think about those same skills in the context of the whole family. There are ways you can help to foster these skills in your family. Take a look at the following techniques that you can practice together:

Validate Strengths and Creative Problem-Solving Attempts

You should not reserve your praise for success alone. Instead, you should be praising *everyone's* attempt and effort, especially when it comes to problem-solving. They might not find the solution right away, but validating and recognizing that they tried will make a world of difference to your family. If your older child tries to soothe their explosive sibling by bringing them their favorite blanket but it is refused, thank them for their thoughtfulness.

Pave the Way for Natural Consequences

It's natural for parents to want to rescue their kids from disappointment and injury, but it's not always what's best for them in the long term. Allow your children to take small, controlled risks and let their outcomes teach them the lesson they need to help build their resilience. It's family night, but no one has done their chores, and the house is a mess. You've let them know all day that if they don't get on top of their chores, then family game night will have to be family clean-up night instead, but still, nothing gets done. Everyone is going to be disappointed that you all have to miss out, but next week, they'll make sure it's all done on time.

Role Model Healthy Coping Openly

When you can verbalize feeling upset or stressed out, you will teach the whole family to articulate their own challenges. But most importantly, if you then demonstrate healthy coping mechanisms like taking calming breaks from work and seeking support when you need it, then you will be role-modeling this for your whole family.

Ask "What If" Questions

This can be a fun game for the whole family. Using the "What if..." as an opening, ask everyone theoretical dilemmas to help them think about their reactions and how to make responsible choices. For example:

- What if you studied really hard but still got a bad grade on a test? What could you do before retaking it to refresh your mood and knowledge?
- What if your best friend had to move to a different town? What could you do to stay in touch and feel better?
- What if you have to speak aloud to the whole class and feel nervous? What positive self-talk or relaxation exercises might be helpful?

Practice Appreciating Present Moments

Set some time aside to spend with your family where you all share gratitude for one another and the things you have in your lives. Discuss your hardest times and the kinds of silver linings you found there—kids often love to listen to their parent's childhood stories. Make family time a frequent and fun time, and let your family environment be a place of peace where everyone can come and breathe when they are facing tough times.

Case Study

The Ioanno family used to coexist alongside each other, like passing strangers in the hallways of their home. Resentment lived among them, and they were all walking on eggshells around the explosive nature of their youngest child, Elaine. When the children argued, the parents would separate them, and resentment grew.

One day, Mrs Ioanno spoke out about how she was feeling as they all sat in silence over breakfast. She told everyone how she felt strained and stressed and that she missed feeling close to her family. By taking the initiative, she role-modeled positive problem-solving and healthy discussion, paving the way for everyone to have their say. They began to practice gratitude for one another and played team-building family games. Over time, they all became more resilient and built better coping mechanisms, benefitting the explosive Elaine and the family as a whole.

Yes, managing an explosive child can be extremely challenging, but as we have learned, it is a journey of growth and learning, and as a family, you can improve your resilience and coping skills and create a better environment for yourselves. Up next, we're going to take a closer look at the family dynamic with tips on how to strengthen relationships and invest time in healthy self-care strategies. Yes, your child is the explosive one, but you need to take care of yourself, too!

CHAPTER 10

THE FAMILY DYNAMIC

The atmosphere in the Leyton household was always so tense you could cut it with a knife. Everyone was weary of Mr. Leyton's fragile temper; Mrs Leyton would stomp around the house passively-aggressively, pointing out all the things on her to-do list, while the children kept themselves locked in their devices, only looking up to eat, drink, and shower. The whole tenuous situation was made ten times worse by the frequent explosive emotional outbursts from the middle child, who had ADHD. Communication among the Leytons was non-existent.

It was only when the Leytons began a parenting course to try and help their explosive middle child with his diagnosis that they really became aware of their family dynamic. They were listening to the group leader explain how to assist their children by using active listening and empathy, and the couple shared a sheepish look. They both realized that they needed to make some changes at home for the well-being of the whole family.

They started by implementing the communication techniques they had learned with the whole family, putting devices and screens away in favor of chatty mealtimes and family movie nights. They bought collaborative board games and learned how to balance the care and attention for all three of their children instead of lending all of their attention to managing the one with explosive behavior. They carved out time for themselves and their relationship and committed themselves to turning the atmosphere in the house inside out.

It took a few months, and there were many slip-ups and setbacks, but six months after that first parenting class, the Leytons sat down with a mug of hot chocolate, each in front of the TV and shared a loving smile with one another when the children burst into the room all at once, each of them excited to get started on the evening's family fun.

STRENGTHENING FAMILY RELATIONSHIPS

Family relationships lie at the core of everything. We carry these early relationships with us into our futures and model all subsequent relationships based on them. They affect our mood and well-being, which can then impact our education and work. Let's take a look at how to strengthen family relationships through building effective communication, creating a supportive environment, and engaging in quality family time.

Building Effective Communication

Consistent open communication demonstrates the unconditional love and respect that a family has for one another. Communication is the foundation on which everything else is built, and this begins with the parents. It has been mentioned again and again already, but as the parent, you model what you want the child(ren) to do. If you do not do it, the child will not do whatever the expectation is (Mettler, 2022). If you are not respectful when you talk to the other parent, then the child won't be respectful when they talk to you. If you want your child to be patient and listen to you, then you need to role-model listening first. At the very core of effective communication is active listening, as we discussed in Chapter 4, and expressing understanding.

Let's take a look at ways you can practice your active listening as a family:

- Play a game of family "spotlight" by taking turns to talk for five minutes about recent updates in your lives. Everyone else has to work on their active listening skills while the speaker is in the spotlight, using eye contact, body language, and facial expressions to engage with the speaker —no interrupting!
- Charades is a great game for practicing nonverbal communication. Take it in turns to choose an emotion and act it out while everyone else guesses what it might be. The exaggerated body language will help everyone to learn to read and express body cues.
- During a family movie night, pause the film and discuss why the characters are making the choices that they are making. What is motivating them? What skill gaps are contributing to their problems? This helps everyone to think about the perspective of others and teaches empathy, which is vital for effective communication.

Creating a Supportive Environment

In Chapter 8, we discussed the role of the physical and emotional environment in managing behavioral challenges with our explosive children. We learned how their physical space can be a trigger for explosive little ones and how to make adjustments for them. We also learned the importance of having a safe, nurturing, non-judgmental environment in helping them work on their emotional regulation skills. Now, let's look at how we can apply similar techniques to create a supportive and non-judgmental space for the entire family:

- **Host family meetings:** These don't have to be every week or even every month unless you want them to be. You could have a family meeting every time there's a big change coming up—"We're hosting Thanksgiving this year; let's come up with a plan together." Or "It's time to redecorate; let's all decide on a new color scheme."
- **Have an appreciation jar:** This is a really cute idea that allows you all anonymously show appreciation for one another. Leave a notepad and pen, and everyone can jot down notes and add them to the jar. Every so often, you can read the notes aloud to the whole family.
- **No-interruption storytelling:** Encourage everyone to use their active listening skills when others are telling a story or sharing something. Use gentle reminders and give everyone the chance to ask questions or share comments after the story.
- **Embrace silliness:** Laugh at your own mistakes, dance when you have too much energy, and make jokes and pull silly faces when someone needs cheering up. Silliness can be a great stress reliever, and laughter encourages everyone to bond and grow closer.

Creating a space for your whole family where they can be their authentic selves without judgment is the ultimate goal. It's about accepting, thanking, and appreciating one another and providing that safe space where everyone can sigh and relax after a long, hard day.

Engaging in Quality Family Time

You may have noticed that all the exercises in this chapter so far have been aimed at you to take part in as a family. There's a reason for that: Quality family time truly is the key to effective communication. It's about building the emotional bond that allows each member to know that they are safe, they are loved, and they are home, regardless of their temperament or explosive nature.

What kinds of activities can you take part in that promote bonding and understanding?

- Movie night!
- Drawing competitions or games like Pictionary. You could even get a YouTube instructional video up, and everyone has to give it a try.
- Jigsaw puzzles can be a lot of fun to do as a family; just make sure you get one that's age-appropriate for your little ones.
- Cooking together has many benefits besides spending quality time—you also get to eat good, nutritious food, and getting the kids involved can help them try new things.

SIBLING DYNAMICS AND FAMILY SUPPORT

Sibling relationships have the potential to be some of the most rewarding relationships of our entire lives. Or they can be the toughest. As parents, you can help your children to lean more toward the former outcome with a little guidance.

Addressing Sibling Needs

When we have an explosive child; they can take up much more of our time than we intend. We may not even notice that we are giving so much extra time and attention to our explosive little one, or we praise our other children for being the "good" ones—meaning less needy. There is a fine line, though, between a child who needs less from their parents and a child who knows they simply won't get what they need. It's a slippery slope, so make sure you are checking in on your other children regularly, even if your explosive child has to take up more of your time and attention for the time being. Be sure to carve out some special time to connect with all your children one-on-one to make sure they aren't slipping through the cracks.

Having strong sibling relationships can be really positive for everyone, not just the explosive child. Unfortunately, resentment is common among siblings, especially if one tends to take up more time and attention than the other.

There are ways you can help your children foster strong sibling relationships that will see them into adulthood. This really begins with knowing and understanding your children as unique human beings with their own needs, likes, and dislikes. It's important to find some common ground to help them connect with each other, even if they are very different people. Perhaps they are both creative, but one likes to paint while the other likes to draw; set them up a little studio at the table where they can both use the tools they prefer alongside each other. Sometimes, siblings bond over a TV show they both love or a celebrity crush. Maybe they both like riding roller coasters. Try to identify and nurture anything they have in common.

Remember, your children didn't choose to exist and live together, so it's important to respect their differences. You can teach them how to compromise and negotiate, which should help ease any resentment or rivalry that might be brewing in the background.

Balancing Attention and Care

As already mentioned, having an explosive child in the family can tip the scales of attention and have a negative effect on the child who feels left behind. This is rarely done intentionally. Dealing with explosive behavior can make you feel like you are constantly putting out fires, but it's important to be proactive about balancing your attention and care, even if your explosive child is more demanding.

Don't minimize or invalidate any feelings of jealousy or neglect; your child is entitled to feel how they feel. Validate how they feel and apologize for your role in it. Then, it is up to you to help them feel valued and loved instead.

To help deal with any feelings of jealousy or neglect, it's important to try to carve out special time just for siblings. Offer them just as much praise and attention as you are giving your explosive child, and thank them for everything they do. You can also try to include siblings as much as possible. If you are practicing role-playing to help your explosive child deal with behaviors or transitions, invite their sibling to join in and play a key role.

Involving Extended Family and Friends

Having an explosive child can feel very isolating. This is often tangled up with feelings of shame and believing you're a bad parent. It can also be tough to be around other families with children who don't have explosive tendencies, and you might secretly find yourself wanting to swap lives with them sometimes. However, isolating yourself and your family will only make matters worse. Getting involved with, educating, and engaging extended family and friends helps to break the stigma around explosive behavior. They can be a source of help and respite if you let them. They can also be effective role models for your child and can even help with balancing the care and attention of your other children.

At first, you may find yourself having to educate your extended family and friends if they haven't had any experience with explosive children before. Chat with them about your child's triggers and any accommodations they need when addressing outbursts; a healthy discussion will prepare them for when it happens and help them understand rather than judge or criticize when it happens. You can also share any positive steps you've made with your child lately—it's not all doom and gloom!

If they don't understand explosive behavior or the associated conditions, then give them a brief rundown. Explain the difference between emotional behaviors versus deliberately acting out, and tell them what they can do to help your family.

When you start involving extended family and friends in your journey with your explosive child, you will find support, love, and acceptance in place of any shame or judgment you placed on yourself. They can help you with your children and even offer you the much-needed childcare for a well-deserved break!

SELF-CARE FOR PARENTS AND CAREGIVERS

Earlier in the book, we touched upon the concept of parental burnout and looked at some core strategies for helping to prevent or draw you out of that cycle. Here, we are going to take a closer look at self-care for parents and caregivers. We're going to develop our understanding of why it is so important, look at some practical self-care strategies, and learn how to build a support network to help you when you need it.

Recognizing the Importance of Self-Care

One of the biggest lessons you have learned so far is that you are a model for your child. They will mirror your actions, and they will learn how to treat themselves based on how you treat yourself.

Running yourself into the ground is not setting a good example for teaching your child relaxation, mindfulness, and regulation now, is it?

Raising an explosive child and dealing with sometimes daily meltdowns can have a huge effect on you physically, emotionally, and mentally. It becomes impossible to nurture your child's emotional well-being because you cannot even nurture your own. You'll snap at them, get angry, and use parenting techniques that don't align with you.

Let's take a look at the common barriers to self-care and ways you can overcome them:

Barrier: I don't have the finances for luxury self-care.

- Who told you self-care has to cost money? If you can't book a spa day, have one at home! Treat yourself to a long, relaxing bath by candlelight—and lock the bathroom door!

Barrier: I don't have time for self-care.

- We all make time to brush our teeth every day or take a shower. You can start small; give yourself 10 minutes a day to sit on your bed to practice your mindful breathing. Over time, you can stretch this out by giving yourself 30 minutes before bed to read or listen to music.

Barrier: I feel guilty making time for myself when there are so many other things to do.

- The laundry isn't going anywhere. Face it; every time you do a load, there's another load waiting. It's not going to end the world if you stop working your butt off for 10 minutes a day, is it? You can even ask for help from your spouse,

friends, or family. Let someone else do your chore while
you take some much-needed me-time!

Barrier: I'm too tired to make time for myself at the end of
the day.

- Did you know that putting yourself to bed early counts as
  self-care? Give it a try and see if it makes you feel good.

Small, consistent steps will mark the start of your self-care journey.
No one expects you to be able to carve out hours at a time for yourself instantly. The key here is simply to notice that even through all
the storms, you matter, too.

Case Study

Emma found herself sitting on the edge of her bed one day,
wondering how she had become such a terrible parent. She was
stressed all the time, the house was an endless mess, the children
ran riot, and everyone was miserable.

She decided she had to get everyone out of this hole—starting with
herself! She knew that the reason she wasn't getting on top of the
housework or being an effective caregiver was because she was
feeling burned out. So, she took it upon herself to carve out some
time to improve her own mental health. After work, she started
sitting on the driveway for 10 minutes before going inside to simply
breathe. This let her leave the stress of work at the door and come
home and be mom. She started going to bed 30 minutes early so she
could read before sleeping, a habit she had lost since having
children.

Very quickly, she began to feel less overwhelmed and better able to
manage everything else. She confidently enlisted the children with
age-appropriate chores, and they got on top of the housework.
Instead of being distracted by the towering pile of laundry or toys

shoved in a pile in the corner, she was able to sit with her children in peace and spend quality time teaching and nurturing them. Emma transformed her caregiving experience through self-care.

Practical Self-Care Strategies

Self-care doesn't have to be time-consuming and complicated! If you think you don't have time for self-care, you're very wrong. Let's take a look at some practical and achievable self-care activities that you can definitely squeeze into your schedule:

- Listen to your favorite podcast while you're running errands. It's good to be able to switch off every now and then. Just make sure you write a list in case you get distracted!
- Dance your way through the housework—or have a five-minute dance party between chores. Think of all the endorphins you'll get moving around your body and lifting up your mood.
- Take a cup of your favorite tea when you get in the bath. You won't want to rush through getting clean and getting out; you'll have to wait for your tea to cool down to enjoy it while you're relaxing.
- If you miss exercising or going to the gym, consider quick HIIT sessions. There are plenty of YouTube videos to inspire you and your kids to join in for some fun and exercise, too.

All these small things paint a much bigger picture: A version of you who is better able to cope with the demands of explosive parenting. Boosting your mental, emotional, and physical health is super important for the well-being of your whole family.

Building a Support Network

Last but not least, let's talk about the importance of building a support network. You know how important it is not to isolate yourself and your family during these tough times especially. Having a support network can make all the difference to parents who are feeling strained and burned out. They don't even have to help you physically deal with your explosive child (although that might be nice!). Simply having someone you can unload to and who will listen to your troubles without judgment or criticism is worth its weight in gold.

You can also find support in online parenting groups. Scrolling through social media and spotting a post from a parent who is struggling with the same things as you can be a huge relief. Eventually, you may even find yourself offering tips and advice to newbie group members.

It really does take a village to raise a family, let alone a family dealing with explosive behaviors.

Clearly, the interconnectedness of family dynamics and self-care is significant to the well-being of everyone, not just explosive children. It's so important to look at the entire picture when a family is having trouble—we see the explosive behavior, and we think that's the only thing we need to deal with when there are so many more layers to this healing and growth journey. Let's turn now to the final chapter, where we will be focusing on the future and the long-term journey of growth.

CHAPTER 11

LOOKING TOWARD THE FUTURE

 Life doesn't get easier or more forgiving; we get stronger and more resilient.

— STEVE MARABOLI

REAL-LIFE SUCCESS STORIES AND CASE STUDIES

Throughout the book, you have encountered real-life success stories and case studies that were included to show you what is possible for you. As you near the end of this experience, let's take a look at a few more to help you look toward the future with excitement and positivity.

Inspirational Success Stories

It was Christmas, and the whole family was at the Mason's house. Jen was a bag of nerves, wondering how her son, Alfie, was going to cope with the visit. The first outburst came within half an hour of everyone arriving; all the children were playing in the playroom when a howl suddenly erupted.

Jen flinched at the sound of Alfie's scream. She quickly excused herself and headed to the playroom to see what she could do. As she stepped into the hallway, she just about caught sight of Alfie storming up the stairs.

"Alfie?" she called. "Where are you going?"

"I'm going to my calm-down spot!" he boomed. "I need my fidgets."

Jen was shocked and pleased. After weeks of trying to get Alfie to use the beautiful calm-down spot she set up in his bedroom, she had all but given up with the technique—his stubborn rage had almost worn her down. But he had been listening and learning through it all, she realized.

The Christmas dinner was far from perfect—when is it ever?—but Alfie took himself to his room every single time an explosion was brewing. He still shouted and seethed on his way up there, but the important thing was that he had learned how to calm and soothe himself so he could come back and join in the festivities again when he was ready.

The school bell rang, and Eloise darted back to her mother, "I need my bag!" she cried.

Ashley let her daughter's backpack slip off her shoulder and handed it to her as she barrelled past. "Wait!" Ashley laughed. "Can I get a kiss or a hug?"

Eloise rolled her eyes and kissed her mom on the cheek quickly before running toward the open doors, ready to start her day.

Another parent stepped up beside Ashley, "Wow, was that Eloise... excited for school?"

Ashley grinned, "She's been like a different child since we started medication."

Max and Raine sat down together the evening after their daughter's graduation and shared a look of deep gratitude and relief.

"We did it," Max said.

Raine wiped away a single tear from her cheek, "Do you remember when we thought she would never even make it to high school because of her behaviors?"

Max squeezed her knee, "I'm so glad we learned how to help her. She's going to do great things in the world."

Shanice took a sip of her champagne.

"How does it feel being the most successful lawyer in the state?" her colleague asked with a grin.

Shanice smiled shyly, "I'm not sure I'm the 'most successful.'"

"How do you do it? What's your secret? I'm not even asking for a friend; I need tips here!" He laughed. "You just go boom, boom, boom, and take the opposition *out*!"

"When I was a kid," Shanice said after a pause, "my teachers told my parents that I would never amount to anything."

"No way!"

"I have ADHD," she admitted. "I was always in trouble. But my parents never gave up on me. They taught me how to reason and problem-solve. They taught me how to control my emotions and how to use my voice. And that's the real secret to my success."

Learning From Case Studies

What are the common key factors that contributed to these inspirational success stories? That's right... it's you, the parents.

The time, effort, and dedication that you have for your child is going to be the catalyst for real, lasting change in their explosive behaviors. The strategies and techniques that you have found in this book will only be as useful as you allow them to be.

True, lasting change comes from consistency, habits, and healthy modeling. Harmony and understanding are available to all families with explosive children.

Diverse Perspectives and Experiences

No family with an explosive child is going to experience exactly the same behaviors and challenges. The important thing is to learn these strategies and techniques, and then you can adapt them to your unique circumstances. What works for the family across the street might not work for your kiddo—and that's okay!

Managing explosive behavior is much like raising a child; you have to accept that things aren't always going to go as planned, and you have to be flexible and resilient in order to teach your children those same skills.

Some children might respond right away, and you'll see behavioral improvements quickly. For other children and often more complex cases, it just takes a bit more time. Your journey with your child is unique, and it's important to remember that as you navigate these times with them.

The most important message here is that you *can* do this, and you *are* good enough.

MAINTAINING PROGRESS AND MANAGING SETBACKS

How long do you think it took you to learn how to add and subtract when you were in school? And how many mistakes did you make in the process? Imagine this journey of overcoming explosive behavior to be a little like that. There are going to be setbacks. Every day isn't going to be sunshine and roses—and that's okay!

Strategies for Sustaining Progress

When it comes to sustaining the progress you have already made, it can help to look back at how far you have come. Each setback might make you feel like the journey isn't worth it, but looking back helps to put that in perspective. As the parent of an explosive child, you might sometimes feel like you are climbing a mountain. Then, when you are going through an explosive challenge, you feel like you fall all the way down to the bottom of the mountain. However, the reality is that you only fell down by 100 feet; you didn't go back to the beginning. For example, your kid is still having explosive episodes... but... they aren't being physically violent toward others anymore. Maybe they are still having meltdowns before school... but... you've been on time for school every day this week.

Let's take a look at some tips for maintaining the positive changes and progress you have made so far (Louisa, 2020; Silver et al., 2016):

- **Consistency, consistency, consistency:** Changing behavior takes an incredible amount of effort, especially when there is resistance like explosive tendencies. This is not something you can put a bandaid on and declare, "All better!" It takes continuous effort. Being consistent in your parenting approach will help your child to depend upon and trust you, and you will see phenomenal results in the end.
- **Routine:** Making sure the techniques you have begun to implement are a part of your daily routine will help you to keep at them. One of the biggest hindrances to progress is when parents slip back into their old habits, so don't let that happen! It might help to have a visual cue for yourself; write a list of how you plan to respond to different behaviors and pin it to your fridge. When my child starts shouting at his siblings, I will take him to his calm corner and sit with him.
- **Regularly review the techniques you are trying to evaluate whether they are working or not:** Is the weighted blanket helping or causing anxiety? Does the calm down corner need a lamp for calmer lighting?
- **Finally, celebrate with your whole family!:** Every milestone, no matter how small, is a cause for celebration. High-fives, stickers, and extra play time all around whenever there's a small win.

Handling Setbacks and Challenges

As mentioned, setbacks are going to happen, and they are nothing to be ashamed of. You can make all the plans and preparations in the world, but things might still go wrong. The most important thing is that you get back up and keep going. Your kid is watching you, and this is such a key lesson for their life in how to manage setbacks and challenges—make them proud.

Your mindset is what is going to dictate your responses here. If you can center yourself and move away from defeatist and disillusioned thoughts, you can motivate yourself, and you can view setbacks as opportunities for learning and growth instead. For example, you packed the travel sensory kit but forgot to take it with you every time you went out. That doesn't mean you should abandon the kit! Put it in the car right now and leave it there so it's always at hand, or leave it somewhere where you can't forget it—in front of the door, or with the shoes, put your keys on top of it.

Evolving With Your Child

Children grow up pretty fast. They move through different developmental phases, which come with different skills and challenges. It's important to adapt your parenting strategies as they grow and change.

If a technique that you used to manage your toddler's explosive behavior stops working at the age of six, it might be time to consider changing your tactics! The table below has some examples of parenting techniques to suit each stage. Remember to tailor this to suit your child, who may have a slightly different timeline:

Age/stage	Techniques for managing explosive behaviors
Toddler (1–3)	• Childproofing the home minimizes sensory/frustration triggers. • Prevent tantrums by avoiding hunger and overtiredness with consistent nap and meal schedules. • Emotionally mirror and validate big feelings during meltdowns. • Embrace repetition around self-regulation skills like deep breathing or positive self-talk.
Elementary (6–10)	• Maintain structured routines while adding visual supports like checklists. • Practice problem-solving academic and social issues collaboratively. • Role-play handling disappointment to build resilience. • Incentivize responsibility and independence with rewards.
Middle school (11–13)	• Respect their need for identity autonomy while providing a listening ear when they need it. • Reinforce organizational supports like wall calendars and tactile fidget devices. • Unpack and discuss complex social dynamics and maturity questions with empathy. • Guide wise decision-making and impulsivity risks logically.
High school (14–18)	• Collaboratively track emotional triggers to head off shutdowns. • Discuss navigating romantic relationships and substance use pitfalls. • Encourage leadership opportunities and boost capability beliefs. • Guide transition planning to ensure support beyond school.

A FUTURE OF UNDERSTANDING AND GROWTH

When you first came to this book, it may have been with the mindset of a person feeling desperate and spiraling. Take a moment now to consider how your mindset has changed since then. You have learned so many techniques and strategies, and you understand your child better than ever. Hopefully, by now, you have an idea of what's possible for your future—it's going to be great!

Envisioning a Positive Future

Take a moment to picture your ideal (realistic!) future. If your child has a diagnosed condition, then picturing a future where they don't have it anymore is unattainable. Instead, picture a future in which their explosive behavior is well-managed.

Next, think about what it's going to take you to get there. This is where you start to set realistic and optimistic goals for yourself and your family. It can be helpful to set both long-term and short-term goals so that you have smaller milestones to work toward and a bigger picture. For example, your big-picture goal might be to have a family holiday—something you've been unable to even consider because of your explosive child's lack of flexibility. The short-term goals to help you get there should involve working on your child's resilience. Work out what the constraints are that you need to work on with your child: Do they struggle sleeping anywhere but their own bed? Then, your first goal should be organizing a sleepover at the grandparent's house, somewhere familiar and nurturing.

Take some time now to think about your long-term and short-term goals. Remember, they should be both realistic and optimistic!

The Role of Community and Society

As the age of traditional parenting passes, parents are turning to implement more conscious and inclusive parenting methods. As a society, we are beginning to learn more and more about how we can positively shape the future of families with explosive children.

When neurodiverse families have a firm presence in society, that helps to normalize and create more inclusive environments for them and others like them. Instead of shame, it's important to show up in the world with pride. All children deserve to be accepted in their wider community, so don't avoid going to the playground just in case your kid has a meltdown. Show up and navigate the situation if it arises. You might just give other parents the confidence to do the same.

Most places are much more inclusive today than they were even five years ago—you can take your kid to the movies for a special autism-friendly screening with low lighting, sound, and more freedom to move around (Dimensions, n.d.).

Continual Learning and Adaptation

As you have probably realized by now, raising an explosive child is not something you can simply fix after a quick parenting course. This is an ongoing journey of education and adaptation for parents and caregivers. Each new stage in their lives is going to bring new challenges, just as it is with other children, although you may have to navigate slightly differently.

At the end of the conclusion, you will find a list of books and further resources that you can explore to continue learning and broaden your understanding of explosive behaviors.

CONCLUSION: REFLECTING ON THE JOURNEY

 *The greater the obstacle, the more glory in overcoming it.*

— MOLIÈRE

I hope that as you close this book, you are feeling empowered and motivated. I hope that you are feeling full of compassion, love, and acceptance for the journey that you are on.

Children who exhibit explosive behavior do not choose to be the way that they are. They have conditions, limitations, and missing skills that can be learned and nurtured. Explosive behavior can be challenging for everyone involved, but it is just that, a challenge that can be overcome.

You should now be equipped with the skills and strategies that you need to tackle this hurdle. Remember that this is a journey, not a race. All families will have different ebbs and flows. Stay in your lane and stay consistent, and you will make a world of difference to your little one's life.

You have learned about compassion and empathy, how foundational they are to your relationship, and how you deal with explosive behavior. We touched upon the limitations of traditional parenting and have spent countless pages learning new strategies to use in its place—strategies that nurture in a more positive way.

You have discovered the importance of finding a support network and how impactful a healthy family dynamic can be. Most importantly, you have seen a better future than your present. You have learned that you, your explosive child, and your family can overcome the hard times with perseverance, consistency, and love.

RESOURCES AND FURTHER READING

Don't forget to seek community and professional support as and when you need it. You are not alone in this. Once you have identified your child's specific challenges and diagnoses that you need support with, you can search online or speak to your pediatrician about reputable organizations that offer tailored guidance for your child's needs. You can also follow social media groups and touch base with fellow parents or call association helplines to speak to a specialist.

To help you on your journey, consider the following books and resources:

Relevant books:

Applied Behavior Analysis by John Cooper, Timothy Heron, William Heward

- *The Explosive Child* by Dr. Ross Greene
- *Good Inside* by Dr. Becky Kennedy
- *The Out-of-Sync Child* by Carol Stock Kranowitz
- *The Whole Brain Child* by Dr. Daniel J. Siegal

- *Meta-Emotion: How Families Communicate Emotionally* by John Mordechai Gottman
- *52 Parenting Principles: How to Bring Out the Best in Your Kids* by Miles Mettler
- *Functional Family Therapy in Clinical Practice: An Evidence-Based Treatment Model for Working With Troubled Adolescents* by Thomas L. Sexton

Supportive websites:

- Understood.org (neurodiversity parenting info)
- Additude Magazine (ADHD focused)
- DaysWithGrey.com (parenting blogs/podcasts)
- CHADD (ADHD focused)

Associations offering guidance:

- American Academy of Child & Adolescent Psychiatry (AACAP)
- Child Mind Institute's Family Resource Center

Congratulations on completing this journey through "Raising an Explosive Child Like a Pro"! You've now equipped yourself with valuable insights and tools to better understand and support children with challenges like ADHD, OCD, or ODD.

But your journey doesn't end here. It's now your turn to pass on the torch of knowledge and assist other parents, grandparents, and caregivers who are seeking guidance in managing explosive behaviors in children.

Your honest review of this book on Amazon can be a beacon of hope for others. Just a few minutes of your time to share your thoughts can make a world of difference. By doing so, you're not just leaving a review; you're guiding someone else toward a path of understanding and empathy.

Here's How You Can Help:

Leave Your Honest Opinion: Scan the QR code below to post your review on Amazon. Your personal experience and insights are invaluable to other readers searching for guidance.

Remember, every word you share helps keep the community of caring for children with explosive behaviors vibrant and supportive.

Your contribution is helping us to spread knowledge, empathy, and understanding to families and caregivers everywhere.

Thank you for being an essential part of this journey. Together, we are making a difference in the lives of children and those who care for them.

- G.G. GrayHaven and the "Raising an Explosive Child Like a Pro" Team

Passing On the Torch of Knowledge

As you move forward, remember the lessons and strategies you've learned. And know that by sharing your experience, you are helping to nurture a community dedicated to raising happy, healthy, and understood children.

Thank You for Making a Difference!

REFERENCES

Abramson, A. (2021, October 1). *The impact of parental burnout*. American Psychological Association. https://www.apa.org/monitor/2021/10/cover-parental-burnout

Achieve Beyond. (2021, December 15). *Antecedent interventions for problem behaviors*. Achieve Beyond. https://www.achievebeyondusa.com/using-antecedent-based-interventions-for-preventing-problem-behaviors/

Ackerman, C. (2019, August). *13 emotional intelligence activities & exercises (incl. PDFs & tools)*. PositivePsychology.com. https://positivepsychology.com/emotional-intelligence-exercises/

ADHD Awareness. (2019, October 16). *MYTH: ADHD is caused by bad parenting*. https://www.adhdawarenessmonth.org/myth-adhd-caused-by-bad-parenting/#:

ADHD Embrace. (n.d.). *Famous people with ADHD*. https://adhdembrace.org/famous-people-with-adhd/#:

American Psychological Association. (2020, February 1). *Building your resilience*. https://www.apa.org/topics/resilience/building-your-resilience

American Psychological Association. (n.d.). *Teaming up: Pointers on successful collaboration with physicians*. https://www.apaservices.org/practice/business/management/tips/collaboration

Andersen, L. S., Magidson, J. F., O'Cleirigh, C., Remmert, J. E., Kagee, A., Leaver, M., Stein, D. J., Safren, S. A., & Joska, J. (2016). Cognitive behavioral therapy. *Journal of Health Psychology, 23*(6), 776–787. https://doi.org/10.1177/1359105316643375

Axtell, P. (2019, April 11). *Make your meetings a safe space for honest conversation*. Harvard Business Review. https://hbr.org/2019/04/make-your-meetings-a-safe-space-for-honest-conversation

Behavioral Innovations. (n.d.). *What is aba therapy & is it right for your child?* https://behavioral-innovations.com/autism-101/what-is-aba/

Barnhill, K., Devlin, M., Moreno, H. T., Potts, A., Richardson, W., Schutte, C., & Hewitson, L. (2018). Brief report: Implementation of a specific carbohydrate diet for a child with autism spectrum disorder and fragile X syndrome. *Journal of Autism and Developmental Disorders*. https://doi.org/10.1007/s10803-018-3704-9

Bennie, M. (2016, February 2). *Tantrum vs autistic meltdown: What is the difference?* https://autismawarenesscentre.com/what-is-the-difference-between-a-tantrum-and-an-autistic-meltdown/

Better Health Channel. (2022, November 8). *Mood and sleep*. https://www.betterhealth.vic.gov.au/health/HealthyLiving/Mood-and-sleep

Beyond OCD. (2018). *Facts about obsessive compulsive disorder*. https://beyondocd.org/ocd-facts

Birth to 5 Matters. (2021). *Self-regulation*. https://birthto5matters.org.uk/self-regulation/

Brown, B. (2018, October 15). *Brene Brown*. Brene Brown. https://brenebrown.com/articles/2018/10/15/clear-is-kind-unclear-is-unkind/

Brown, B. (2018, October 15). *Clear is kind. Unclear is unkind*. Brené Brown. https://brenebrown.com/articles/2018/10/15/clear-is-kind-unclear-is-unkind/

Campos, M. (2020, January 30). *Food allergy, intolerance, or sensitivity: What's the difference, and why does it matter?* Harvard Health. https://www.health.harvard.edu/blog/food-allergy-intolerance-or-sensitivity-whats-the-difference-and-why-does-it-matter-2020013018736#:

Carpenter Rich, E., Loo, S. K., Yang, M., Dang, J., & Smalley, S. L. (2009). Social functioning difficulties in ADHD: Association with PDD risk. *Clinical Child Psychology and Psychiatry*, *14*(3), 329–344. https://doi.org/10.1177/1359104508100890

Caspi, A., Elder, G. H., & Bem, D. J. (1987). Moving against the world: Life-course patterns of explosive children. *Developmental Psychology*, *23*(2), 308–313. https://doi.org/10.1037/0012-1649.23.2.308

Centers for Disease Control and Prevention. (2006). *Tips for talking with parents*. https://www.cdc.gov/ncbddd/actearly/pdf/parents_pdfs/tipstalkingparents.pdf

Centers for Disease Control and Prevention. (2022, September 13). *Sleep hygiene tips - sleep and sleep disorders*. https://www.cdc.gov/sleep/about_sleep/sleep_hygiene.html

Centers for Disease Control and Prevention. (2022, August 9). *Data and statistics about ADHD*. https://www.cdc.gov/ncbddd/adhd/data.html

Children and Adults with Attention-Deficit/Hyperactivity Disorder (CHADD). (n.d.). *About*. https://chadd.org/about/

Chapman, A. L. (2006). Dialectical behavior therapy: Current indications and unique elements. *Psychiatry (Edgmont (Pa. : Township))*, *3*(9), 62–68. https://www.ncbi.nlm.nih.gov/pmc/articles/pmid/20975829/pdf/?tool=EBI

Childcare. (n.d.). *Responding to challenging behaviors*. https://childcare.gov/consumer-education/responding-to-challenging-behaviors

Child Mind Institute. (2021, October 6). *About individual education programs (ieps)*. https://childmind.org/article/about-individual-education-programs-ieps/

Cleare, A. (2023, February 22). *15 ways parents can support children to do well at school*. Anita Cleare. https://anitacleare.co.uk/ways-parents-can-support-children-to-do-well-at-school/

Cleveland Clinic. (2017). *Attention deficit disorder (ADHD)*. https://my.clevelandclinic.org/health/diseases/4784-attention-deficithyperactivity-disorder-adhd

Cleveland Clinic. (2023a, June 9). *Emotional dysregulation*. https://my.clevelandclinic.org/health/symptoms/25065-emotional-dysregulation

Cleveland Clinic. (2023b, February 22). *Attention-deficit/hyperactivity disorder (ADHD)*.

from https://my.clevelandclinic.org/health/diseases/4784-attention-deficithyperac tivity-disorder-adhd

Cleveland Clinic. (2023c, February 26). *Autism spectrum disorder.* https://my.cleveland clinic.org/health/diseases/8855-autism

Connor, D. F., Newcorn, J. H., Saylor, K. E., Amann, B. H., Scahill, L., Robb, A. S., Jensen, P. S., Vitiello, B., Findling, R. L., & Buitelaar, J. K. (2019). Maladaptive aggression: With a focus on impulsive aggression in children and adolescents. *Journal of Child and Adolescent Psychopharmacology, 29*(8), 576–591. https://doi.org/ 10.1089/cap.2019.0039

Cooper, J.O., Heron, T.E., & Heward, W.L. (2020) *Applied behavior analysis.* Pearson, 3rd Ed.

Cuncic, A. (2022, November 9). *What is active listening?* Verywell Mind. https://www. verywellmind.com/what-is-active-listening-3024343

Danielson, M. L., Bitsko, R. H., Ghandour, R. M., Holbrook, J. R., Kogan M. D., Blumberg S. J. (2018). Prevalence of parent-reported ADHD diagnosis and treat-ment among U.S. children and adolescents, 2016. *Journal of Child and Adolescent Psychology, 47*(2), 199-212 https://www.tandfonline.com/doi/full/10.1080/15374416. 2017.1417860

Deckelbaum, L. (2021, December 1). *Mindfulness, the bedrock of emotional intelligence.* Mindsmatter. https://mindsmatter.com/mindfulness-emotional-intelli gence/#:~:text=So%20how%20do%20we%20teach

Dimensions. (n.d.). *Autism friendly cinema screenings.* https://dimensions-uk.org/get-involved/campaigns/autism-friendly-cinema-screenings/#:

Dvir, Y., Ford, J. D., Hill, M., & Frazier, J. A. (2014). Childhood maltreatment, Emotional dysregulation, and psychiatric comorbidities. *Harvard Review of Psychiatry, 22*(3), 149–161. https://doi.org/10.1097/hrp.0000000000000014

Early Intervention Foundation. (2018). *What is early intervention?* https://www.eif.org. uk/why-it-matters/what-is-early-intervention

Ehmke, R. (2017, October 17). *Teaching kids about boundaries.* Child Mind Institute. https://childmind.org/article/teaching-kids-boundaries-empathy/

Elliott, A. (n.d.). *Emotional regulation.* The Child Psychology Service. https:// thechildpsychologyservice.co.uk/theory-article/emotional-regulation/

Empathic listening. (n.d.). Skills You Need. https://www.skillsyouneed.com/ips/ empathic-listening.html#:

Feehan, M., McGee, R., Stanton, W. R., & Silva, P. A. (1991). Strict and inconsistent discipline in childhood: Consequences for adolescent mental health. *British Journal of Clinical Psychology, 30*(4), 325–331. https://doi.org/10.1111/j.2044-8260. 1991.tb00953.x

Fletcher, J. M. (2013). Alternative approaches to outcomes assessment: Beyond psychometric tests. *Pediatric Blood & Cancer, 61*(10), 1734–1738. https://doi.org/10. 1002/pbc.24824

Fongaro, E., Picot, M. C., Stringaris, A., Belloc, C., Verissimo, A. S., Franc, N., & Purper-Ouakil, D. (2022). Parent training for the treatment of irritability in children and adolescents: a multisite randomized controlled, 3-parallel-group, evaluator-blinded, superiority trial. *BMC Psychology, 10*(1). https://doi.org/10.1186/s40359-022-00984-5

Fowler, P. (2018, January 11). *Breathing techniques for stress relief*. WebMD. https://www.webmd.com/balance/stress-management/stress-relief-breathing-techniques

From chaos to calm: Effective behaviour management strategies for the classroom. (2023, May 16). Routledge. https://www.routledge.com/blog/article/behaviour-management-strategies-for-the-classroom

Family and Social Services Administration. (2015). *Assistive supports and therapies*. https://www.in.gov/fssa/ddrs/files/AssistedSupports_BS_BT_ABC_V2.pdf

Gershoff, E. (2002). Is corporal punishment an effective means of discipline? *APA*. https://www.apa.org/news/press/releases/2002/06/spanking

Gottman, J. M., Katz, L. F., & Hooven, C. (1996). Parental meta-emotion philosophy and the emotional life of families: Theoretical models and preliminary data. *Journal of Family Psychology, 10*(3), 243–268. https://doi.org/10.1037/0893-3200.10.3.243

Gottman, J.M., Katz, L.F., & Hooven, C. (1997). *Meta-emotion*. Psychology Press.

Grajek, M., Krupa-Kotara, K., Białek-Dratwa, A., Sobczyk, K., Grot, M., Kowalski, O., & Staśkiewicz, W. (2022). Nutrition and mental health: A review of current knowledge about the impact of diet on mental health. *Frontiers in Nutrition, 9*(943998). https://doi.org/10.3389/fnut.2022.943998

Greene, R. W. (2018, February 6). *10 rules for dealing with the explosive child*. ADDitude. https://www.additudemag.com/how-to-deal-with-an-explosive-child-tips/

Greene, R. W. (2021). The explosive child [sixth edition]: A new approach for understanding and parenting easily frustrated, chronically inflexible children (4th ed.) [e-book]. Harper Paperbacks.

Growing Early Minds. (2019, November 5). *How to set healthy boundaries with your kids*. Growing Early Minds. https://growingearlyminds.org.au/tips/how-to-set-healthy-boundaries-with-your-kids/

Guarnotta, E., & Troy, B. (2023, August 2). *Functional family therapy: What it is, cost, & what to expect*. Choosing Therapy. https://www.choosingtherapy.com/functional-family-therapy/

Hofmann, S. G., Asnaani, A., Vonk, I. J. J., Sawyer, A. T., & Fang, A. (2012). The efficacy of cognitive behavioral therapy: a review of meta-analyses. *Cognitive Therapy and Research, 36*(5), 427–440. https://doi.org/10.1007/s10608-012-9476-1

Hvolby A. (2015). Associations of sleep disturbance with ADHD: implications for treatment. *Attention deficit and hyperactivity disorders, 7*(1), 1–18. https://doi.org/10.1007/s12402-014-0151-0

Jack, D. (2023, October 6). *Understanding explosive parenting: A practical guide for*

parents.   Medium.   https://medium.com/@DicksonJackCoachandBlogger/under
standing-explosive-parenting-a-practical-guide-for-parents-23f4b5d3ccfb

John Hopkins Medicine. (n.d.). *Oppositional defiant disorder (ODD) in children*.
Hopkins   Medicine.   https://www.hopkinsmedicine.org/health/conditions-and-
diseases/oppositional-defiant-disorder#:

Kaminski, J. W., & Claussen, A. H. (2017). Evidence base update for psychosocial
treatments for disruptive behaviors in children. *Journal of Clinical Child &
Adolescent Psychology*, *46*(4), 477–499. https://doi.org/10.1080/15374416.2017.1310044

Kearney, S. (2021, May 6). *5 warning signs your child struggles with self regulation*.
Children in Motion. https://childreninmotion.com/2021/05/06/signs-child-strug
gles-with-self-regulation/

Kellogg, M. (2022, February 9). *How and why to measure emotional intelligence*. Criteria
Corp.   https://www.criteriacorp.com/blog/how-and-why-to-measure-emotional-
intelligence#:

Kennedy, B. (2022). *Good inside a guide to becoming the parent you want to be*.
Harpercollins Publishers Limited.

Kids Health. (n.d.). *ADHD Medicines (for teens)*. Kids Health. https://kidshealth.org/
en/teens/ritalin.html#:

Koseva, N. (2023, August 23). *Children with ADHD and routines: Building healthy struc-
tures*. The ADHD Centre. https://www.adhdcentre.co.uk/children-with-adhd-
and-routines/

LEARN Behavioral. (2019, October 24). *Precursor behaviors*. [Video] YouTube.
https://www.youtube.com/watch?v=GFF6izSpLVw

LinkedIn. (2023, December 22). *How can you balance structure and flexibility in the classroom?*   https://www.linkedin.com/advice/o/how-can-you-balance-structure-flexibil
ity-classroom-mcvzf#:

Kinne, J. (2022, July 13). *Co-regulation*. The OT Toolbox. https://www.theottoolbox.
com/co-regulation/

Kling, J. (2017, October 11). *Difference between iep, bip, and 504*. Alternative Teaching.
https://www.alternativeteaching.org/iep-bip-and-504-plans/

Lindberg, S. (2007, December 11). *What is emotional numbing?* Verywell Mind. https://
www.verywellmind.com/emotional-numbing-symptoms-2797372

Li, P. (2020, December 4). *Angry child: How to deal with explosive behavior*. Parenting
for Brain. https://www.parentingforbrain.com/anger-issues-in-kids/#:

Lopes, V. (2023, October 9). *Angry kids: Dealing with explosive behavior*. Child Mind
Institute.   https://childmind.org/article/angry-kids-dealing-with-explosive-behav
ior/#:

Louisa. (2020, January 24). *Ten tips for maintaining progress towards your goals*. My Self-
Help Habit. https://www.myselfhelphabit.co.uk/2020/01/24/ten-tips-for-maintain
ing-progress-towards-your-goals/

Lovering, N. (2021, September 29). *Treating ODD: What are my options?* Psych Central.

https://psychcentral.com/disorders/oppositional-defiant-disorder-treat ment#home-remedies

Lovevery, T. (2022, June 24). *5 co-regulation tips to help your toddler manage their feelings.* Lovevery. https://lovevery.com/community/blog/child-development/5-co-regula tion-tips-to-help-your-toddler-manage-their-feelings/

Low, K. (2023, March 28). *8 simple school strategies for students with ADHD.* Verywell Mind. https://www.verywellmind.com/help-for-students-with-adhd-20538#:

Maraboli, S. (n.d.). *Resilience quotes.* Goodreads. https://www.goodreads.com/quotes/ tag/resilience

Mayo Clinic Staff. (2018, January 6). *Autism spectrum disorder - Diagnosis and treatment.* Mayo Clinic. https://www.mayoclinic.org/diseases-conditions/autism-spectrum-disorder/diagnosis-treatment/drc-20352934#:

Mayo Clinic Staff. (2019a, June 25). *Attention-deficit/hyperactivity disorder (ADHD) in children - Symptoms and causes.* Mayo Clinic. https://www.mayoclinic.org/diseases-conditions/adhd/symptoms-causes/syc-20350889#:

Mayo Clinic Staff. (2019b, September 18). *Intermittent explosive disorder - Symptoms and causes.* Mayo Clinic. https://www.mayoclinic.org/diseases-conditions/intermittent-explosive-disorder/symptoms-causes/syc-20373921#:

Mayo Clinic Staff. (2020, September 15). *Mindfulness exercises.* Mayo Clinic. https://www.mayoclinic.org/healthy-lifestyle/consumer-health/in-depth/mindfulness-exer cises/art-20046356

Mayo Clinic Staff. (2022, October 7). *Temper tantrums in toddlers: How to keep the peace.* Mayo Clinic. https://www.mayoclinic.org/healthy-lifestyle/infant-and-toddler-health/in-depth/tantrum/art-20047845

Mayo Clinic Staff. (2023, November 21). *Obsessive-compulsive disorder (OCD) - symptoms and causes.* Mayo Clinic; Mayo Clinic. https://www.mayoclinic.org/diseases-condi tions/obsessive-compulsive-disorder/symptoms-causes/syc-20354432

Mead, E. (2019, September 26). *What is positive self-talk?* Positive Psychology. https:// positivepsychology.com/positive-self-talk/

Mental Health Foundation. (2022, January 25). *Diet and mental health.* Mental Health. https://www.mentalhealth.org.uk/explore-mental-health/a-z-topics/diet-and-mental-health

Mettler, M. (2022). *52 parenting principles how to bring out the best in your kids.* Morgan James Publishing.

Merriam-Webster. (n.d.). Discipline. *In Merriam-Webster.com dictionary.* https://www. merriam-webster.com/dictionary/discipline

Merriam-Webster. (n.d.). Empathy. *In Merriam-Webster.com dictionary.* https://www. merriam-webster.com/dictionary/empathy

Micanti, F., Iasevoli, F., Cucciniello, C., Costabile, R., Loiarro, G., Pecoraro, G., Pasanisi, F., Rossetti, G., & Galletta, D. (2016). The relationship between emotional regulation and eating behaviour: a multidimensional analysis of obesity psychopathology. *Eating and Weight Disorders - Studies on Anorexia, Bulimia and Obesity, 22*(1), 105–115. https://doi.org/10.1007/s40519-016-0275-7

Millacci, T. S. (2022, January 18). *16 activities to stimulate emotional development in children*. PositivePsychology.com. https://positivepsychology.com/emotional-development-activities/

Miller, C. (2016, April 19). *Choosing a parent training program*. Child Mind Institute. https://childmind.org/article/choosing-a-parent-training-program/

Miller, G. (n.d.). *What is a behavior intervention plan?*. Child Mind Institute. https://childmind.org/article/what-is-a-behavior-intervention-plan/

Mind. (2019, May). *Treatment for OCD*. https://www.mind.org.uk/information-support/types-of-mental-health-problems/obsessive-compulsive-disorder-ocd/treatment-for-ocd/

Mind. (2022, March). *Managing stress and building resilience - tips*. https://www.mind.org.uk/information-support/types-of-mental-health-problems/stress/managing-stress-and-building-resilience/

Mind Tools Content Team. (2022). *Active listening*. Mind Tools. https://www.mindtools.com/az4wxv7/active-listening

Mind Tools Content Team. (n.d.). *Empathic listening*. Mind Tools. https://www.mindtools.com/a8l9jo8/empathic-listening

Molière. (n.d.). *Overcoming obstacles quotes*. Goodreads. https://www.goodreads.com/quotes/tag/overcoming-obstacles

Montessori, M. (n.d.). *Maria Montessori quotes*. Quote Fancy. https://quotefancy.com/quote/981188/Maria-Montessori-The-environment-itself-will-teach-the-child-if-every-error-he-makes-is

Morin, A. (2021, March 27). *6 parenting strategies for raising emotionally intelligent kids*. Verywell Family. https://www.verywellfamily.com/tips-for-raising-an-emotionally-intelligent-child-4157946

Morin, A. (2020, October 1). *Effective solutions parents can use for common child behavior problems*. Verywell Family. https://www.verywellfamily.com/common-child-behavior-problems-and-their-solutions-1094944

Morin, A. (2021, March 27). *How to manage misbehavior with discipline without punishment*. Verywell Family. https://www.verywellfamily.com/the-difference-between-punishment-and-discipline-1095044#:

Mrug, S., Hoza, B., & Bukowski, W. M. (2004). Choosing or being chosen by aggressive–disruptive peers: Do they contribute to children's externalizing and internalizing problems? *Journal of Abnormal Child Psychology, 32*(1), 53–65. https://doi.org/10.1023/b:jacp.0000007580.77154.69

Murray, L. (2014). *The psychology of babies*. Hachette UK.

National Autistic Society. (2020, August 14). *Stimming - a guide for all audiences*. Autism. https://www.autism.org.uk/advice-and-guidance/topics/behaviour/stimming/all-audiences

National Autistic Society. (n.d.). *Professionals involved - a guide for parents and families*. Autism. https://www.autism.org.uk/advice-and-guidance/topics/diagnosis/profes

sionals-involved/parents-and-families

Nelsen, J. (2018, November 21). *About positive discipline*. Positive Discipline. https:// www.positivediscipline.com/about-positive-discipline

National Health Service. (n.d.). *RDaSH leading the way with care developing skills in children*. https://camhs.rdash.nhs.uk/wp-content/uploads/2021/04/NL-Emotion-regu lation-e-leaflet-02.21.pdf

National Health Service England. (2022). *Resources to improve the sensory environment for autistic people Sensory-friendly resource pack*. https://www.england.nhs.uk/wp-content/uploads/2022/10/B0467_i_Sensory-friendly-resource-pack_.pdf

National Health Service. (2021, February 4). *Helping your child with anger issues*. https://www.nhs.uk/mental-health/children-and-young-adults/advice-for-parents/ help-your-child-with-anger-issues/

National Society for the Prevention of Cruelty to Children. (2022, September 9). *How to have difficult conversations with children*. https://learning.nspcc.org.uk/safe guarding-child-protection/how-to-have-difficult-conversations-with-children/

Ogundele, M. O. (2018). Behavioural and emotional disorders in childhood: A brief overview for paediatricians. *World Journal of Clinical Pediatrics*, 7(1), 9–26. https:// doi.org/10.5409/wjcp.v7.i1.9

O'Neal, C., Meyering, K., Tan, S. C., Wong, E. L., Lee, V., Babaturk, L., & Estevez, G. (2019). Emotion and stress regulation magic tool box. https://education.umd. edu/sites/default/files/uploads/Emotion%20and%20Stress%20Regulation% 20Magic%20Tool%20Box.pdf

Paley, B., & Hajal, N. J. (2022). Conceptualizing emotion regulation and coregulation as family-level phenomena. *Clinical Child and Family Psychology Review*, 25. https:// doi.org/10.1007/s10567-022-00378-4

Parekh, R. (2022, June). *What is ADHD?* American Psychiatric Association. https:// www.psychiatry.org/patients-families/adhd/what-is-adhd

Pelini, S. (2023, January 13). *Inconsistent parenting - Raising-independent-kids*. Raising Independent Kids. https://raising-independent-kids.com/inconsistent-parenting/

Pietro, S. (2016, February 2). *Angry kids: Dealing with explosive behavior*. Child Mind Institute. https://childmind.org/article/angry-kids-dealing-with-explosive-behav ior/

Play Therapy UK. (2021). *What is play therapy?* Play Therapy UK. https://playtherapy. org.uk/what-is-play-therapy/

Positive Action Staff. (2020, October 14). *20 evidence-based social skills activities and games for kids*. Positive Action. https://www.positiveaction.net/blog/social-skills-activities-and-games-for-kids

Psychology.org Staff. (2022, February 15). *What is art therapy?*. Psychology.org. https:// www.psychology.org/resources/what-is-art-therapy/

Psychology Today Staff. (n.d.). *Emotional intelligence*. Psychology Today. https://www. psychologytoday.com/us/basics/emotional-intelligence

Rosanbalm, K.D., & Murray, D.W. (2017). *Caregiver co-regulation across development: A practice brief*. OPRE Brief #2017-80. Washington, DC: Office of Planning, Research, and Evaluation, Administration for Children and Families, US. Department of Health and Human Services. https://fpg.unc.edu/sites/fpg.unc.edu/files/resources/reports-and-policy-briefs/Co-RegulationFromBirthThroughYoungAdulthood.pdf

Segal, J., Smith, M., Robinson, L., & Shubin, J. (2023, February 28). *Improving emotional intelligence (EQ)*. HelpGuide. https://www.helpguide.org/articles/mental-health/emotional-intelligence-eq.htm

Selby. (2023, August 18). *Cultivating empathy and resilience: Reflective journal prompts for social-emotional learning*. Everyday Speech. https://everydayspeech.com/sel-implementation/cultivating-empathy-and-resilience-reflective-journal-prompts-for-social-emotional-learning/

Selhub, E. (2022, September 18). *Nutritional psychiatry: Your brain on food*. Harvard Health Blog; Harvard Health Publishing. https://www.health.harvard.edu/blog/nutritional-psychiatry-your-brain-on-food-201511168626

Sexton, T., & Turner, C. W. (2010). The effectiveness of functional family therapy for youth with behavioral problems in a community practice setting. *Journal of Family Psychology, 24*(3), 339–348. https://doi.org/10.1037/a0019406

Sexton, T. L. (2011). *Functional family therapy in clinical practice*. Taylor & Francis Group.

Sherin, J. E., & Nemeroff, C. B. (2011). Post-traumatic stress disorder: the neurobiological impact of psychological trauma. *Dialogues in Clinical Neuroscience, 13*(3), 263–278. https://www.ncbi.nlm.nih.gov/pmc/articles/PMC3182008/

Siegel, D. J., & Bryson, T. P. (2012). *The whole-brain child*. Bantam Books Trade Paperbacks.

Silver, S. A., McQuillan, R., Harel, Z., Weizman, A. V., Thomas, A., Nesrallah, G., Bell, C. M., Chan, C. T., & Chertow, G. M. (2016). How to sustain change and support continuous quality improvement. *Clinical Journal of the American Society of Nephrology, 11*(5), 916–924. https://doi.org/10.2215/cjn.11501015

SLW. (2022, October 27). *How do I create smoother transitions for my child?*. Social Learning Works. https://sociallearningworks.com/child-development/how-do-i-create-smoother-transitions-for-my-child%EF%BF%BC/

Sonuga-Barke, E. J. S., Becker, S. P., Bölte, S., Castellanos, F. X., Franke, B., Newcorn, J. H., Nigg, J. T., Rohde, L. A., & Simonoff, E. (2022). Annual research review: Perspectives on progress in ADHD science – from characterization to cause. *Journal of Child Psychology and Psychiatry, 64*(4). https://doi.org/10.1111/jcpp.13696

Stormshak, E. A., Bierman, K. L., McMahon, R. J., & Lengua, L. J. (2000). Parenting practices and child disruptive behavior problems in early elementary school. *Journal of Clinical Child Psychology, 29*(1), 17–29. https://www.ncbi.nlm.nih.gov/pmc/articles/PMC2764296/

Suni, E. (2020, August 14). *What is sleep hygiene?* (N. Vyas, Ed.). Sleep Foundation. https://www.sleepfoundation.org/sleep-hygiene

Synapse. (n.d.). *Understanding challenging and complex behaviours*. Synapse. https://synapse.org.au/fact-sheet/understanding-challenging-and-complex-behaviours/

Thomas, R., Mitchell, G. K., & Batstra, L. (2013). Attention-deficit/hyperactivity disorder: are we helping or harming? *BMJ, 347*(nov05 1), f6172–f6172. https://doi.org/10.1136/bmj.f6172

Thompson, S. (2021, October 22). *How to Improve your Communication Skills, with Key Resources*. VirtualSpeech. https://virtualspeech.com/blog/improve-communication-skills

Turner, L. (2023). *The Importance of a daily schedule for a child with ADHD*. Twinkl. https://www.twinkl.co.uk/blog/the-importance-of-a-daily-schedule-for-a-child-with-adhd

Unity Point Health. (n.d.). *A therapist explains why we shut down when flooded with big emotions*. Unity Point. https://www.unitypoint.org/news-and-articles/a-therapist-explains-why-we-shut-down-when-flooded-with-big-emotions#:

Urwin, S., & Holroyd, T. (n.d.). *What is animal-assisted therapy? | Types of therapy*. BACP. https://www.bacp.co.uk/about-therapy/types-of-therapy/animal-assisted-therapy/

Vandekerckhove, M., & Wang, Y. (2017). Emotion, emotion regulation and sleep: An intimate relationship. *AIMS Neuroscience, 5*(1), 1–17. https://doi.org/10.3934/Neuroscience.2018.1.1

Valiente, C., Eisenberg, N., Haugen, R., Spinrad, T. L., Hofer, C., Liew, J., & Kupfer, A. (2011). Children's effortful control and academic achievement: Mediation through social functioning. *Early Education & Development, 22*(3), 411–433. https://doi.org/10.1080/10409289.2010.505259

Waller, R. (2015). *Dropping the baby and other scary thoughts*. Hachette UK.

Wesarg-Menzel, C., Ebbes, R., Hensums, M., Wagemaker, E., Zaharieva, M. S., Staaks, J. P. C., van den Akker, A. L., Visser, I., Hoeve, M., Brummelman, E., Dekkers, T. J., Schuitema, J. A., Larsen, H., Colonnesi, C., Jansen, B. R. J., Overbeek, G., Huizenga, H. M., & Wiers, R. W. (2023). Development and socialization of self-regulation from infancy to adolescence: A meta-review differentiating between self-regulatory abilities, goals, and motivation. *Developmental Review, 69*, 101090. https://doi.org/10.1016/j.dr.2023.101090

Webb, J. (2023, October 3). Childhood emotional neglect hampers emotional intelligence. *Psychology Today*. https://www.psychologytoday.com/us/blog/childhood-emotional-neglect/202306/childhood-emotional-neglect-hampers-emotional-intelligence

WebMD Editorial Contributors. (2008, September 25). *Food dye and ADHD*. WebMD. https://www.webmd.com/add-adhd/childhood-adhd/food-dye-adhd

WebMD Editorial Contributors. (n.d.). *What to know about parental burnout*. https://www.webmd.com/parenting/what-to-know-about-parental-burnout

Whitbourne, K. (2003, February 10). *Oppositional defiant disorder*. WebMD. https://www.webmd.com/mental-health/oppositional-defiant-disorder

Wilde, J. (2012). *Understanding and managing children's behaviour through group work ages 5-7*. Jessica Kingsley Publishers.

Woudstra, I. (2022, October 31). *7 tips for creating safe spaces for speaking out*. Voice at the Table. https://www.voiceatthetable.com/blog/7-tips-for-creating-safe-spaces-for-speaking-out/

Yale Medicine. (n.d.). *Anger, irritability and aggression in kids*. Yale Medicine. https://www.yalemedicine.org/conditions/anger-issues-in-children-and-teens#:

Young Minds. (n.d.-a). *How to talk to your child about mental health*. YoungMinds. https://www.youngminds.org.uk/parent/how-to-talk-to-your-child-about-mental-health/

Young Minds. (n.d.-b). *School anxiety and refusal | Parents' guide to support*. YoungMinds. https://www.youngminds.org.uk/parent/parents-a-z-mental-health-guide/school-anxiety-and-refusal/

Your Headspace Mindfulness & Meditation Experts. (n.d.). *Sleep hygiene tips*. Headspace. https://www.headspace.com/sleep/sleep-hygiene

Zauderer, S. (2023, September 15). *Trigger analysis In ABA: Definition & examples*. Cross River Therapy. https://www.crossrivertherapy.com/aba-therapists/trigger-analysis#:

www.ingramcontent.com/pod-product-compliance
Lightning Source LLC
Chambersburg PA
CBHW020237130626
46549CB00005B/1938